LIFE AFTER ABORTION

A WOMAN'S JOURNEY TO HEALING AND GOD'S HIDDEN MIRACLE PLACED WITHIN

Ashlee Mincer

All Scripture in this publication is taken from the NEW AMERICAN STANDARD BIBLE®, Copyright ©1960, 1962, 1963, 1968, 1971, 1972, 1973, 1975, 1977, 1995 by *The Lockman Foundation.* Used by permission.

This is a work of nonfiction. Many names have been changed for privacy purposes.

Copyright © 2020 by Ashlee Mincer

Loved (5.5x8.5) Self-Publishing Template © 2017 Renee Fisher https://www.reneefisher.com

Cover Design by Nelly Murariu, pixbeedesign.com

ISBN: 978-0-578-65508-6

I felt as though I was walking hand-in-hand with the writer, Ashlee Mincer, through each season of her life. I was in awe of the personal relationship she has formed with Christ Jesus. This book unveils how God the Father has planned out with great purpose every detail of our lives.

—Brandy Holmes
Ohio

Ashlee put a face and heart on my conviction in praying weekly before an abortion facility. After reading her story, I realize that she wrote her story so that people will take action and help another. My heart has gone through a conversation for those who went through what Ashlee went through, and are going through today, with an unplanned pregnancy.

—Carol Fox
Ohio

Raw, real, redemptive... This book takes you through a lot of emotions but has completely changed my perspective. I am no longer pro-choice but am pro-life. I'm so glad to finally read a book that doesn't hold back the reality and truth. I would recommend this book to all ages and genders but especially young women.

—Jess, 34 yrs

As I finished reading *Life After Abortion*. I thought about all the broken girls and women who have been through an abortion. Ashlee truly has shown that there is forgiveness. I recommend this book to anyone suffering post abortion.

—Yvette Rash
Clients Coordinator at Heartbeat of Ottawa
County Pregnancy Center-Port Clinton,Ohio

A beautiful story of brokenness and redemption! Ashlee displays bravery in sharing her personal experiences that so many are afraid to speak of, from the darkness that she endured to recognizing that if you give it all to God, He will not fail you. From someone who works for a pregnancy center and has helped facilitate abortion healing retreats, I've seen the work of healing and forgiveness firsthand. Ashlee's story is a testimony for so many of those individuals who walk through our doors, a story that has proven that rock-bottom does not mean it's the end but a beautiful start.

—Marisa Moya
Center Director at Heartbeat Hope Medical of
Fremont, Ohio

Ashlee's story is a powerful story full of heartbreak, despair, and God's unfailing promises and love. Her bravery and obedience to share and to continue moving forward in her healing have had such a tremendous impact in my own healing journey. She has given voice to the pain of post-abortive women, who many times don't feel they deserve to be heard. I have no doubt Ashlee's story will fill many hearts full of understanding and compassion. It is a testimony that tells of the proof of the power in the cross and will be sure to provide hope, healing, and courage to those who have experienced or been affected by the heartbreak of abortion.

— Anonymous, post-abortive

The struggles and trials Ashlee has experienced in her post-abortive healing journey are expressed beautifully in her book. Whether experiencing post-abortion trauma firsthand or watching from the sidelines, the trauma is real. I recommend her book to anyone who needs to more deeply understand the burdens one carries when weighed down by such a debilitating secret.

A story of redemption, a story of what can lead to decisions and different turns on a path that someone may least expect. Because of God's grace, He can take those paths and change them into a completely different destination for a person. This is exactly what occurred on Ashlee's path. This book unfolds into that path, where the reader can feel the ruts, stones, and even branches in the way. But then God makes the path smoother, clearer to see by removing the branches. I am so grateful I was able to read these words!

Dedication

To my son Samuel, who left this earth far too early, yet not without a God-ordained purpose. I love you so much. I will forever be your voice until we meet in heaven. What a glorious day that will be.

Until then, momma hopes to make you proud by leaving an impact on this earth for the most innocent without a voice—the unborn.

Table of Contents

Introduction

It was the cool, early morning on March 22, 2015, when I heard a whisper from God. This specific whisper I had heard before. It was once again the Holy Spirit ushering me in to *write*.

The exciting day was here. Our little family of four would venture onto the road mapped with too many miles to count from our home state of Ohio to vacation in Myrtle Beach, South Carolina. I set aside the soft yet strong assuring voice that I knew well deep within my soul. There was no time to sit and meditate deeper into the morning. We needed to get moving, getting everyone ready, packed, and out the door for the long trip.

With both kids buckled, snuggling in with their blankets and pillows, I made sure I had my necessities within arm's reach. Tucked snug in my bag was my pink Bible filled with sticky notes and highlights, my journal, pens, the current book I was reading, yarn, and, last but not least, a crochet hook.

Craig filled up the gas tank in town and made sure to stop at the McDonald's drive thru. He wanted everyone taken care of, with Lily and Landon's tummies full and me relaxing in the passenger seat with coffee in hand as we set out on our long excursion in the wee hours of the morning.

As I sipped the hot sweet deliciousness mixed with sugar and creamer, we listened to worship music and gazed at the sunrise peeking over the horizon. Craig looked at me with a smile as he reached for my hand and intertwined our fingers tightly together. The sweet moment seemed to make time stand still. I could sense his relief at being able to shut off work mode for a week to enjoy this much-needed quality family time.

The bright hues of pink, orange, and yellow that filled the sky in fiery contrast made it easy to get lost reminiscing on the broken yet beautiful journey my Heavenly Father had taken me on five months prior. I reflected with a thankful heart on not only the last five months of a miraculous work, but the beautiful broken road that He had been working all for my good throughout my entire life.

After being deep in thought for quite some time on the drive, I reached down and pulled out my Bible, eager to hear more from God. What I wasn't expecting was the loud and clear confirmation in scripture of my assignment to *write*.

Habakkuk 2:2

"'Record the vision and inscribe it on tablets, that the one who reads it may run.'"

"Craig, you know how God has been telling me to write? Listen to what I just read. God is speaking to me to write a book," I said with excitement.

As our eyes met, he didn't say one word, which was fine with me. His beaming grin said everything, confirming without a doubt that God was continuing to move in my life.

Although I was very excited with this word and confirmation, I didn't necessarily feel qualified to do what I was being asked. I am a stay-at-home mom from a small town with no college degree. I never imagined I would write a book. In fact, for many seasons—about four years to be exact—I wrestled with whether

I could fulfill God's plan and purpose. Writing did not come easy for me. Yet, when you receive a clear call and instruction from the Father, "no" is just not an option.

We were near our final destination in Myrtle Beach when God made it clear He wasn't finished with ending the day on a grand note. Suddenly, the words sprung forth, boldly declaring the clear call to action.

Jeremiah 30:2

"'Write all the words which I have spoken to you in a book.'"

It was obvious in this season what God wanted me to write. It was time to tell the story of the path He had led me down to help crack open the thick, hard callous that covered a deep, dark wound I had kept hidden inside for fifteen years. The last five months had been an incredible journey that landed me on my knees in surrender, crying out for forgiveness and healing, and gratefully receiving an unexpected miracle.

When God intercedes on our behalf in our moments of deepest despair, He doesn't want us to keep it to ourselves. I knew this without a doubt as I remembered what I wrote in my journal a day after the Lord tore the veil from my blinded eyes and placed the most precious miracle gift in my hands.

Journal Entry 11/12/2014

"The story of this miracle is not over. It is just unfolding. My son's story was not meant to be kept silenced. I pray for the time I share this story, my story, my God, God's miracle. I have a lump in my throat holding back tears. God, You would not perform a miracle for it to be kept in a box and closed. Jesus, I

> love you and want to come to You empty-handed and offer my
> life in complete surrender."

When I wrote "my story" in my journal, I had no idea that healing from my abortion was not even close to completion. In fact, after these five months it would be another four years of continued walking by blind faith into God's will that would lead my story back full circle (Romans 8:28).

I could have never made up nor imagined for myself the places my Heavenly Daddy would take me. I especially was unaware of the extent and gravity of grief, guilt, shame, and trauma I was still carrying—yes, even after the heaven-on-earth miracle graciously given to me.

Our healing here on earth coincides with our willingness to take ownership in saying yes, to take those frightening steps toward the unknown to continue forward. The great Author of my life was continuing to rewrite my story as I walked in faith and total dependence on Him.

Ephesians 3:20

"Now to Him who is able to do far more abundantly beyond all that we ask or think, according to the power that works within us."

Chapter 1 – Home is Where Your Story Begins

I grew up in a small town bordered by water on the north. Living right along Lake Erie means gift shops selling "Lake Life" signs, hopping local coffee shops, and seagulls soaring and singing from above. Even in the long, dreary, winter months, the serenity of their song continues.

There is always a sense of relaxation when the beach is just a short distance away and in view as you drive through town. The town pier parking lot next to the lighthouse is where you can find many locals soaking in the serenity of the ripples in the water on their lunch breaks.

I like the simplicity of a quaint, down-to-earth, small town. Big cities get me in a bit of a nervous state with the congested traffic, lack of parking, and the "busyness" of navigating through the day.

Although I do enjoy traveling with my family, my biggest solace is to be home with my husband and children enjoying the simple things in life. I can get lost in a book, journaling, or behind a blank canvas with paintbrush in hand. Being creative allows my brain to shut off the troubles or disappointments of the day and shift my mind to just "be still."

Flowers are another passion of mine as I attended floral design school. Before becoming a stay-at-home mom, I enjoyed working in the floral business for about six years. I found myself falling in love not only with the different colors and aromas but with each intricate detail of the petals. The creation of flower arrangements soothed my soul in a way that refreshed my mind with peace and tranquility.

When my husband and I found out we were having our first child, a daughter, it was inevitable that we would name her after a flower. "Lily Grace" would be the perfect name for her.

Growing up, I didn't truly have an understanding of the Bible, church, or God. My family went to church when I was younger, yet there were years of inconsistency. I never really remembered anything I was taught. Other than knowing baby Jesus in a manger, an ark full of animals, and a man being swallowed by a whale, I didn't understand the good news of the Gospel. The idea that Jesus would die on the cross for me was incomprehensible to me. I never knew nor felt His love and mercy. An understanding of "how" to have a relationship with Him was far out of my grasp. My limited understanding came in the form of going to church, memorizing the Lord's Prayer, reading my Bible, and throwing in some small prayers before bed.

When I was 10 years old, my mom, dad, older sister, and I moved to a city about thirty minutes away to the city where my dad was employed. This was the season when things started to change for me physically. The childhood I had known would never be the same.

At 10 years old, I had become very sick, eventually being diagnosed with an autoimmune disease called JRA (juvenile rheumatoid arthritis). The carefree child who loved to run, play, and do cartwheels, just like my peers, was now bedridden with swollen and stiff joints. Chronic fatigue set in as my immune system attacked itself.

After two years living close to my dad's work, my family decided to move back to our hometown that we missed. The local newspaper ran an article about my experience living with arthritis when I was 12. "'There is room in this world for everyone.' Young girl tries to cope with arthritis."

I was a sixth grader at the time when I had my picture taken with my golden retriever on our front steps—the very steps of the house God would eventually lead me back to a few decades later, bringing my story full circle.

> Growing up I didn't truly have an understanding of the Bible, church or God.

I was put on a strong medication that was classified as a cancer drug. These types of medications became part of my weekly routine in order to function on my own and experience any quality of life. In my case, the joint damage was so severe that it can never be restored. However, the strong medication slowed its rapid growth.

My physical disability certainly affected my self-esteem and how I saw myself. Reminders were always present that I was "different." Physically, I was unable to do the same activities as everyone else.

Two years after my diagnosis, my rheumatologist found a medication called methotrexate that would put my body into remission. This was around the same time when we decided to move back to our little hometown on the lake.

A new beginning was taking place. Being reunited with friends, a new house right in town, and with my body and joints feeling almost normal again certainly seemed to signal that a new beginning was about to flourish.

Life was looking hopeful again as I experienced more happy days than painful, depressing days. Yet, another curveball was right around the corner with many more painful, relentless obstacles ahead.

When I reached junior high, I began to experience bullying. The harassment would not stop, and I couldn't get away from it no matter how hard I tried. The bullying combined with my already-low self-esteem from my physical disability pushed me into a deep depression, to the point of attempting suicide. This was the first onset of clinical depression for me. Something had happened in my mind that was beyond my control.

My doctors started me on antidepressants soon after my suicide attempt. Once the medication started to get into my system, I began gaining back my mind that had held me captive. The days looked brighter, and I felt happiness once again. The medication didn't take my problems away, but it did help me get through them better.

I maneuvered into high school, trying to discover where I fit in. As part of the tennis team and excelling in art, I felt like I had "a place" for the most part.

The summer before my junior year, I met a guy who showed great interest in me. The more we spent time together, the more I felt wanted and loved. I clung to this relationship because it helped me feel good about myself. Having him helped me forget about my peers who bullied me and who I had to face every day at school.

Matthew and I were high school sweethearts, falling head over heels in love for one another. I should have been seeking my identity in Christ, His love for me, and what He knew was best for me. Instead, Matthew was everything to me, fulfilling the needs and desires I had.

Despite the clear warning from my rheumatologist that the baby would have serious birth defects from my medication, I found myself pregnant at the age of 18, right after I graduated. My careless actions of having unprotected sex eventually caught up with me.

My parents were on vacation when I took the pregnancy test after missing my period, and dread consumed me as I worked up the courage to call them with the news. I was prepared for their disappointment over my actions, but I wasn't quite prepared for the plans that would be discussed.

While I was still dealing with the shock of discovering I had a baby growing inside me, I was told there was no other option but to terminate the pregnancy. Despite my parents being pro-life, the fear of the unknown pushed them to a very hard resolution, without considering any other options. The doctor's strong warning had convinced them that if I became pregnant, there would be no other option because the baby wouldn't be healthy and disfigured. My reckless behavior and poor choices had put them in a very frightening place.

In an instant, my world came crashing down. It was thought to be the "only option" at the time, yet in reality, it was the worst choice that could have been made for me.

I can't recollect if, in my naivety, I had even heard the term abortion before. However, the harsh truth of that word was pretty clear as I knew it was to terminate this pregnancy.

Proverbs 16:9

"The mind of man plans his way, but the Lord directs his steps."

The story I share now is not my own. In the beginning, yes, but after the abortion, God rewrote my story, bringing me to the road of redemption in a way that only He could orchestrate. He is truly the Great Author over my life, and all the glory is His. God eventually revealed through the pain, loss, and trauma exactly why it all had to happen. There *was* a purpose through all of it. Nothing would be wasted.

Now at the end of the journey, I can confidently say that I understand His plan, but it was very difficult to accept my past during the healing process.

I was told there was no other option.

To accept my mistakes and failures that resulted in lifelong guilt and regret.

To accept the loss of a child I was desperately still holding onto in immense sadness and grief.

By God's grace, I have finally found healing and come to a place of confidence in who I truly am in Christ Jesus. My Heavenly Daddy allowed me to experience His plan to turn my brokenness into something more beautiful than I ever could have imagined. He showed me what could be turned around for good when I stopped hiding from my past, when my broken soul surrendered to the place it was declared done and finished—*at the foot of the cross.*

Beauty rose up from the ashes, sculpted into a masterpiece more amazing than my imagination could ever dream. In the throne room of heaven, there are dimensions of God we've never experienced before, things we have never seen nor thought He would have for us. Blueprints were written into our life record before we were even yet conceived, predestined by His mighty hands.

Psalm 139:16

"Your eyes have seen my unformed substance; and in Your book were all written the days that were ordained for me, when as yet there was not one of them."

How amazing is it to truly take in and feel the truth of those words deeply and personally? The details unfold slowly, but His fingerprints rest upon them.

When we set our hearts on His faithfulness, we can look back on the journey and see His perfection amongst chaos. We can see how we were held and cherished through it all.

My Savior reached His mighty hand deep in my heart to pull out what was lost, who I loved, and who I still love and long for—*my aborted child.* He revealed a new identity for me. This identity would not come in form of a title such as floral designer, wife, or mother. It would come as my true identity in Christ Jesus and what that truly means and looks like.

Despite fallen areas in my life, destiny was set. I saw my life as a frustrating jigsaw puzzle. Many times, I wanted to give up trying to fit the pieces together. My life was in 1000 pieces of failure, sin, brokenness, death, hope, surrender, deep healing, and blessing. The complicated pieces that were too much to put together by my own wisdom or strength would fit perfectly together by God's grace and provision through the years, slowly and intricately displaying His beautiful picture of purpose in my life.

This is my abortion story and my journey to healing and redemption.

Chapter 2 – The Clinic

The early days of summer 1999 were supposed to be filled with work, making that "good money," soaking in the sun rays with friends at the beach, and ending the day at the movies while the sun set. This was the last carefree summer to soak up every minute before my classmates and I would step foot into the real world of college, trade school, or full-time jobs.

Instead of living out the best summer of my life after graduation, I found myself on an airplane to a destination that would change who I was forever. Alone and petrified, battling morning sickness, I was flying from my home state of Ohio to Florida to have an abortion. The signs and symptoms of sickness I was experiencing from the human life growing inside of my womb made my situation all the more real, but this was the decision.

From the moment I told my parents the news, a turbulent whirlwind of fear came in, posing as an urgent "crisis" situation. The intense realization that the baby would have serious birth defects put things in motion very quickly as if "it" needed to get done as soon as possible. It was a "the-earlier-the-better" kind of thing, yet there was absolutely nothing that felt "better" in this situation I was facing. I didn't want to end the life of my baby. The amount of loneliness I experienced was swallowing me up. My whole being was drowning in anguish, with nowhere to turn and no one else to talk to. This clinic was the "solution" for my crisis pregnancy.

That day at the abortion clinic became a blur. My mind blocked out much of it from the trauma. Yet, I distinctly remember specific moments that will never leave me.

As I gazed up at the green palm tree branches swaying to and fro in the sunlight, there was a sense of secrecy as I was lead to a back door in the early morning on that hot, humid summer day for a surgical abortion. There was nobody around outside, just the silence of the morning as the warmth of the sun beat down on those waving palm leaves. But no amount of sunshine, tropical warmth in the air, or beach and ocean could take away even a smidge of the darkness I felt that day.

I do remember the clinic being clean, professional, and white—just white, from the walls to the exam chair I was lying on to the nurse's attire. Like a blank sheet of paper, so too was my mind. BLANK. NUMB. The cleanliness and "professionalism" was a façade hiding the gruesome truth and reality of what took place there every day—not just the horrific violence to the most innocent but also to their mothers.

Distinctively deep in my gut, I knew this wasn't right. My mind grasped naturally that this was much more than just a "medical procedure."

Because I was 18, I was the only one who could legally sign the papers, even though I don't remember doing so. I didn't want to be there. Maybe I was young and naïve to think the medication I was on wouldn't affect the baby. The mind-numbing feeling as the pen met the paper was a huge blow to my heart, leaving it completely shattered, broken and bleeding in anguish. This was the only option offered to me as I stood at the check-in, signing my child's death sentence. It is an indescribable feeling. In that pivotal moment, that signature forced me to believe the lie that my child had no worth.

As I lay on the reclining exam chair, it reminded me of being at the dentist except it had cold, metal stirrups at the bottom. This appointment was a far cry from a regular teeth cleaning. My life was going to forever change on that chair. I was devastated, broken, and traumatized before anything even took place.

While sitting in that small room at the abortion clinic, shock that I had landed myself here consumed me. How and why I had gotten myself into this situation tore me up inside, but the answer to those questions was evident. I went against God's Word by having sex before marriage.

It felt like a nightmare with the unspeakable outcome that was coming no matter how much I wrestled it in my mind. I had made such a careless mistake getting pregnant on this strong medication, and being given no other option but to follow through with the abortion left me feeling completely helpless and alone.

I wasn't informed of a local pregnancy center. I didn't even know that such a place existed. Yet, there was one right down the street from my house. There was no ultrasound done to discover if there was anything wrong with the development of my baby. There was no medical diagnosis in a picture to somewhat "justify" why I was ending the life of my child.

I never got to see the first picture of my baby. The visual was hidden at the clinic because they didn't want to take the chance that I might have changed my mind or discovered strength to fight for the life inside me. Even if the abortion clinic didn't see a problem with the development of the baby, I know now they wouldn't have told me. The paper was signed and money already in their hands. Ultimately, the abortion took place based completely on my doctor's warnings about would most likely happen. There was no actual evidence to confirm it at the time.

Incredible grief and sadness over my child who I desperately did not want to be separated from forever consumed every part of me. A dark, looming cloud of guilt hovered over my head for not protecting my baby, and that guilt would continue to haunt me long after I left that clinic.

Due to the emotional and mental trauma, as well as being sedated for the procedure, much of the experience was blocked from my memory. The memory that stands out from that day was lying on that cold, white chair in a gown. My mind-numbing gaze was set on the IV in my right hand that would send the light anesthesia to my veins.

> In that pivotal moment, that signature forced me to believe the lie that my child had no worth.

The moment was coming when I would go to sleep and wake up barren, no longer a mother. Lying there felt like an invisible prison I could not escape from, the place where a life would end and a mother's life would change forever.

The nurse went over everything with me step by step as if it was supposed to bring me some sort of comfort. Her instructions were short and sweet.

"Ashlee, soon I will administer the medicine into your IV," she stated.

"You will go to sleep shortly. You won't feel anything or remember anything," she stated with strong reassurance in her voice.

I responded with a silent nod.

Her words sounded so gentle yet pierced my heart all at the same time. Her delicate voice and words surely "sounded" reassuring. In that moment I mistakenly believed her.

How could I not believe her?

This place and people who worked there obviously knew what they were doing, right? They helped women in a pregnancy crisis.

Deep down, I knew it wasn't right as I tried my hardest not to let the tears flow. Putting on a brave face, forcing myself to bottle all the emotions swirling inside, was the only choice I had in that moment.

I would understand later that the nurse's words were such a lie. They were the enemy's lies in a sweet whisper, just like to Eve in the Garden of Eden.

Genesis 3:4

"You surely will not die"

It will be over with soon, I kept reassuring myself. I could get through this. Relief would soon be in sight. *You will be fine, Ashlee. Just breathe.*

In the end, the enemy won that day as I became barren in my womb and inside my soul.

About 15-20 minutes after waking and able to keep some fluids down, I was released. My discharge instructions were rest, no strenuous activity, and no soaking in water such as swimming or baths for a certain period of time. Ibuprofen was okay to take for pain. The nurse warned I might have some bleeding but that was normal.

They might have prepared me for what was going to happen to me physically, but not psychologically. How does one go through such a devastating traumatic experience only to be sent back out into the world like nothing even happened? But that is what the post-abortive are left to do.

Walking out of the clinic and through the parking lot with sadness, I glanced over. An older lady, probably a grandmother, caught my attention as she sat on the curb. Her somberness was evident, sitting in silence with a sign propped against her legs. Already deflated, I quickly heard the nurse escorting me out say, "Don't look at her." I kept my head down to the ground while passing her. Honestly, that was easy to do after what I had just done.

The lady didn't say anything. She knew what had already taken place. In those mere seconds of exiting the parking lot, I saw on her face and through her body language a sense of defeat. My escort had made me feel as if this lady was going to bombard me with condemnation, but, surprisingly, it was the total opposite. She, too, felt defeated that day, unable to save yet another baby and mother.

> In the end, the enemy won that day as I became barren in my womb and inside my soul.

I have no memory of what exactly she had on her sign, but deep down I knew what she had on that sign was truth. After the abortion, I often thought of that little old lady on that curb, wishing I would have had a chance to run into her before walking into the clinic. If so, would my child be here today? It was a thought that I would ponder many times, only to find out in the end that encounter was never meant to be.

Years down the road, early in my healing journey, I really wrestled with why God didn't use this woman as a divine intervention to help me. *God, why couldn't You have put her in my path at the right time instead of when it was too late? Surely You are a good God. So why didn't you intervene on my behalf?*

In my younger years, I had no knowledge of the truth that God is indeed in the thick of things, the in between and the future. We can be blinded by our circumstances that diminish our inner knowledge that God is working all things for good, even when we are hit with devastating, tragic circumstances that are out of our control. For me, it would be a long road before God would answer that difficult question of "Why?"

Losing my child in the manner I did left me wanting to block everything out, as if it never happened. I didn't want to feel the unbearable pain inside that was consuming every fiber of my being. It was too intense.

When I returned home after the abortion, it was unspoken but clear that this wasn't to be talked about. Abortion is just not a subject of conversation. We see it so much in our society today, but even back in the day when abortion first became legal, it has always been the hidden, secret sin. In turn, women are taught very early that we don't need healing from what we endured as a result of the choices we made or were coerced to make. This is why so many suffer in silence.

Life resumed as if it never happened. It felt like I was expected to leave it all behind, but how was I supposed to go on with life after what I had done?

There was no roadmap in sight to give me direction. The precious, innocent life lost was gone forever. I would never know if I had a boy or a girl. Never get to see their beautiful face, hold and comfort them. My child's identity was erased forever. On top of this loss Matthew and I broke up as soon as I returned home.

Days were very low-key after returning home, especially regarding friends. I didn't have much of a social life, but not long after being home, I got an unexpected knock on my door. To my surprise, it was a friend who was in my Advanced Placement art class my senior year, but we had actually grown up together.

Opening the door as we stood there together, I could sense his compassion. It was evident he had heard through the grapevine what had happened.

"I am sorry for what happened. I heard," Jake said, displaying heartfelt compassion.

"So, you got plans tonight?" he asked with a hopeful smile.

A small sense of hope started to emerge. Yet, I still felt the urge to recoil. I was hesitant to step out of the house where I was hidden and secure from the outside world.

> Life resumed as if it never happened.

"Some of us are hanging out at a house on the lake. Do you want to come hang out for the night? Come on, it will be fun. It would do you some good to get out." Jake was persistent and not taking no for an answer in an effort to get my mind off of the hardships of life.

I desperately needed an escape at this point, and the last of my hesitation vanished with his persistent pleading. Hanging out with friends at a party, drinking, and letting loose felt like just what the doctor ordered.

That night, I met a guy who had a very sweet and caring personality. Kurt and I hit it off quickly. No doubt the alcohol and marijuana had a lot of influence, but I was also ready for a new beginning. We started hanging out a lot after that night and soon started dating.

Although I felt a great fondness for Kurt, deep inside I was still trying to mask all of the pain I was carrying. Desperately trying to move on from the past, I let myself get lost in this new love relationship pretty quickly. The connection between us was also fueled after hearing Matthew had cheated on me while I was in

Florida having the abortion. I was devastated all over again when I returned home to hear this news.

Now, looking back, who knows how he was handling the abortion. Fathers are usually forgotten about in these situations, but the reality is that fathers are often affected just as much by abortion as the mothers.

Regardless of what pushed Matthew to cheat on me, we were now headed in different directions. For me, I was headed toward a point when my circumstances would clash. The truth would be evident that no amount of alcohol, marijuana, or love and affection from a guy could fill the deep, dark void within.

Chapter 3 – He Leaves the Ninety-Nine

I became very angry and defiant as my depression started to spiral down fast. In only two months, I was in a state of deep clinical depression. Everything was filled with darkness. Nothing mattered anymore.

The deep black hole of depression had my mind sucked in, anchored with heavy weights wrapped in locked chains, never to be free. My mind was stuck in a vicious cycle of mental torment.

The day that I decided I couldn't handle the pain anymore was a day I was supposed to go to a counseling appointment with my father. Along with showing signs of depression, I was also displaying a lot of anger and unruly behavior. I thought it was too late. I was too far gone to go on with life anymore. There was nobody who could try and save me at this point, or so I thought.

I refused to go to the appointment. Lying in bed, my mind filled with darkness, silent tears fell as I stared at Kurt's pictures taped to my wall. I cared about him a lot, but he couldn't save me. I just lay there as silent tears dripped, consumed with utter despair over the irreversible loss and complete hopelessness.

Despite my refusal to go to the appointment, my father still decided to go see the counselor. As soon as he drove off, I took an extra set of keys to my car, which I was grounded from using, and took off in the opposite direction.

I wanted to leave all the pain behind. My mind was set. There was no going back, no second guessing. I never thought to leave a note. The pain just needed to end and soon.

In that moment, I didn't know exactly how or where. What I knew without a doubt was that I was following through and nothing would stop me. Soon the pain would be gone. I just didn't want anyone involved or hurt.

John 10:10

"The thief comes only to steal and kill and destroy; I came that they may have life, and have it abundantly."

August 23, 1999, two months after the abortion, on a country road about thirty minutes away from home, I drove my car into a tree to end my life. The enemy fought hard, almost having his way with me that day. Death was present for a moment, but miraculously life was brought back into my broken body and deflated lungs. God was watching over me at the moment of impact with His angels ready on standby. I didn't know there was a divine purposeful plan over my life or what I was truly worth. I can only imagine the spiritual battle going on that day.

It wasn't my time. Nothing would stop the unique heavenly design over my life. My Savior's mighty hand reached from the heavens down into the mangled maroon Buick Skylark, operating the paramedic's hands to breathe life back into me. My Creator boldly displayed that He was not done with me yet. There was neither trauma too extensive nor wreckage so great that could override what was already written for me.

Bones in my face shattered to pieces from smashing into the

> I wanted to leave all the pain behind. My mind was set.

steering wheel since my car had no air bag. The impact was so intense that the steering wheel bent out of place. My right ankle and elbow were also crushed as my foot was under the brake pedal and my legs were stuck under the dashboard. Both lungs had collapsed, and when it seemed matters couldn't be any worse, the car started to catch on fire.

"I was inside the house and I heard the impact and knew something hit pretty hard," said Wally, a neighbor close to the accident. He said he looked outside and saw that the car had hit the tree and was on fire. He called 911 and ran out with a fire extinguisher and put out the fire.

"That old fire extinguisher did the job," said Wally. "I haven't needed it for twenty-seven years, but I needed it today."

He said as he worked on the fire, I was coherent, yelling for someone to help get me out of the car, which he couldn't.

"I could see she had a lot of injuries, so I wanted to keep her as calm as possible, but she kept yelling, 'Get me out, get me out!'" stated a former nurse who lived on the other side of the road. I don't remember any of this as she held my hand trying to calm and comfort me.

Another neighbor who also attempted to help was a retired ophthalmologist who once ran an emergency room in Wichita, Kansas. All of these details I have no memory of but learned from the article in the newspaper.

The odds were against me, yet God was already performing miracles until the paramedics arrived. Although I stated I didn't want to involve anyone, regrettably I truly did. I wasn't thinking about who would find me to witness such a gruesome, horrific scene. I wasn't thinking about how I would hurt my family. Deep clinical depression just wants the pain inside to end, unfortunately feeling there is no other way out.

The paramedics, along with the Jaws of Life, worked with endless determination for an hour to free me. Removing me was difficult because of the heavy damage the car received. It made it hard to find something for the Jaws of Life to pry against. They were forced to intubate me from inside of the car when both lungs had collapsed. That's the point to where I was gone. The two one-inch scars on either side of my rib cage are reminders of where Mercy knew my name. The scars mark forever reminders that nothing is impossible for God.

I was transported by helicopter to Cleveland Metro Hospital in serious condition. The teams of doctors were nothing short of amazing, keeping me alive while quickly addressing my broken body. Reconstructive surgery was done on my right ankle and elbow as well as my face. Most can't tell by looking at me now that my face consists of 6 plates and 34 screws. After a week, by the grace of God, I came out of the coma and quickly realized my plan had miraculously not been successful.

Why?

Why would God fight so hard to save me?

Although I didn't have a relationship with God, it was evident a miracle happened from a higher power that day. The doctors knew that as well, astonished that I pulled through and survived.

Sitting in my hospital bed, I was in deep thought of the gravity of what I had done. As my eyes slowly scanned up and down my body, digesting the sight of serious injuries I caused, I knew suicide would never be an option again.

The thought was scary. I had so much uncertainty about how I was going to go on with life now. I became the girl who survived running her car into a tree. Many in my town, friends at my school and their parents, knew about my struggles with depression and my first suicide attempt. All I could think was, "Look what I've done to myself," self-conscious of who might figure out the inevitable.

How my car managed to crash into a tree along with the odd location was not discussed. The focus was on getting me healed and stronger to be able to go home. My parents knew deep down what had happened. My past struggles, depression, and suicide attempt made this no news flash.

I could see this was coming when a hospital psychologist walked into the room with her clipboard and pen in hand, ready to ask me questions. These questions I had heard before, questions intended to lead up to a confession that this "accident" was intentional. Depression and suicide were the last things on my mind to talk about after surviving what I had along with the major injuries I needed to heal from. Home was where I wanted to be. If I confessed to what I had done, it would be a no-brainer that I would be staying even longer for intense evaluation and suicide watch.

I do remember leaving the house and my intention up to the point of near the location where the accident occurred, but that is where my memory ends. Seeing the tree, the moment of impact and being conscious inside the car were things I would never remember.

As the psychologist's questions intensified, I shut down and lied, making it clear that I didn't remember anything from that day. Surviving that accident was certainly a loud wakeup call. Deep down, I felt there must be some reason why I survived. There was no reason medically why I was still here. But I was.

When I was discharged from the hospital, I was in a wheelchair for about a month until I could get the casts off my leg and arm to start physical therapy. Upon arriving home from the long drive from the hospital, I found a blessing waiting. There was a beautifully built wooden ramp leading up to the steps of my front door. The father of a friend I played tennis with took the time to build the ramp for me as a gift. That gesture definitely helped me to know that people cared for me, that I could continue to heal and fight this battle now living as a suicide survivor.

It wasn't long after most of my body had healed that I was smoking marijuana and drinking again to drown out everything I had experienced that summer. Here I was again trying to rebuild my life, searching to discover who I was after an abortion and severe suicide attempt. This cycle of constant trials seemed like a broken record throughout my life. From the age of 10, I felt I was always battling something that affected my identity. I never saw myself stripped of everything that I thought "defined" me to be able to see myself the way my Creator always had.

I was seeking the world for my identity and worth rather than seeking God. All I knew to do was to mask the pain and trauma with substances that left me high, numb, and empty inside. I wouldn't discover until 18 years later that I was experiencing symptoms of post-abortion syndrome. I didn't know then that abortion truly does affect a woman. Abortion is not simply a quick fix to whatever circumstances deem it justifiable.

Kurt and I continued dating for a short period of time after the car accident. He hadn't known suicide was a part of my past, and soon after I returned home from the hospital, he was warned by people to "be careful" of me. I was being labeled as a fragile girl who was crazy enough to kill herself.

I eventually retreated back to the relationship with my baby's father, Matthew. For some reason, I couldn't let go of that relationship even though it turned unhealthy. Even after he moved across the country, I had a very hard time getting over him.

After Matthew moved away permanently, the partying continued and the drugs became stronger. I drowned myself in anything I could to prevent thinking or facing the reality of my life. I put myself in some really bad situations, even landing myself at drug dealers' houses. I acted as if I didn't have a care in the world, recklessly drinking while driving many times. It's a miracle I never hurt anyone or landed myself in jail. I was a train wreck, a complete mess inside.

> I was seeking the world for my identity and worth rather than seeking God.

Needing to feel some sense of control, I started to be very restrictive with my diet, leading into a full-blown eating disorder. Anorexia and diet pills led into bulimia, where I was binging and purging several times every day. My life had been so out of control, I felt my weight was the one thing I could control. However, it really had control over me, to the point I couldn't stop even if I desperately wanted to. I was very thin, sick, and still tremendously broken inside.

When I was 15 years old in high school, I had started to babysit for a friend of the family. A strong bond was developed for three years before my life started to spiral out of control. Spending time and continuing to build a strong bond with this special family kept me grounded in some way despite the aftermath from my poor choices. They were an important part of my life no matter what I was going through.

During the season of hidden self-destruction, I received a devastating phone call that one of the children from this family was in a car accident with his mom and baby sister. Tragically, 3-year-old sweet little Cole, who had been adopted into this family, didn't make it. This was very close to the time my baby would have been born. Later in my story, God would reveal that Cole had in fact passed away just two days before my baby would have been due.

Seven months had passed from the time of the abortion to Cole's unexpected death. At this point, Matthew and I were still together for a short season before he moved the following year across country. Matthew held me on the couch as I cried out in utter distress, "I want my baby back. I just want my baby back." Speaking those words secretly allowed my inner being to grieve my own child as well. Truth was, I was crying out to *my* baby.

The grief I was experiencing was doubled. These two great losses filled me with piercing pain I had never experienced before in my life. I was struggling because God saved me from my car accident that I purposefully caused five months prior. Yet, this sweet little boy was not saved to live the long life still ahead of him. As I type these painful words, they also hold true for my aborted child.

Cole and his siblings had visited me after I was released from the hospital. He and his older brother, Michael, made me a box with pictures of them on all sides. Inside was a precious recording of Cole's sweet little voice saying "get better soon." My heart was shattered wishing more than anything that *he* could have had the opportunity to get better soon.

How could this be happening?

This loss and goodbye seemed unreal. Walking into the funeral home, I could barely stand on my own. My parents took hold of each arm, holding me up. I almost couldn't muster enough strength for this farewell, but I needed to. Cole's mother let me tuck a bracelet with angels on the beads in the front pocket of his denim overalls, close to his heart.

After that day, my intense grief was in form of not only a deeply-wounded soul, but anger as well. I had lost not just one but now two important children in my life at a young age. I had experienced an abortion, surviving a severe suicide attempt, and losing another child close to me, all within seven months. I was angry with people, angry with life, and yes, very angry with God. Making any sense out of anything, and especially God, was impossible at this point. The path of self-destruction continued, numbing myself anyway I could for a few years.

There eventually came a time when the drugs and alcohol became too much. I was tired of the life I was living. My mind and body were simply worn out. I wanted out of this life that offered me nothing good, leaving me completely empty inside. The only way to do that was to totally detach from the friends I was hanging out with. I could see the person I had become and hated the reflection I saw looking back at me in the mirror. Despite not really loving myself, I had enough self-respect left to want a better life. I needed a drastic change.

In this season, my parents were also separated. I was living with my mom in a small apartment. This was when I started to seek a relationship with God. I figured it was time after seeking everything else failed me. I didn't quite know how, so I started with something that I loved to do—*art*.

Worship music played as my paintbrush met the blank canvas. I spent hours clipping out inspirational words and quotes, along with crosses, angels, and flowers.

God's creation was uplifting and helped me forget about anything negative. Art was an outlet that easily enabled me to be close to my Maker. Art allowed me to shut out the world, the pain, and the reality of what my life had been. This period of time was just the beginning of my journey with Him. I was thirsting for something more than what I knew.

Also during this time, I started taking some classes at a community college while continuing to work in the floral business. But as far as a career, I had no idea of what I wanted to do in life. Working in the floral business was my passion, something I knew I was good at. It brought me a lot of joy even though it didn't pay a whole lot. As it's commonly said, "Money can't buy happiness." Despite an eating disorder that I continued to battle, I was starting to feel hope and happiness again.

Although I could start to see a light of hope at the end of the tunnel, trying to envision rebuilding my life again was hard to do. I still carried invisible, deep wounds that I hadn't faced or dealt with properly.

Where was my place in life after the chaos and destruction of my past?

Who would want to be with a person like me, with a past like mine?

Chapter 4 – The Beginning of the Story is Not the End

I had always longed for a healthy relationship, someone who would embrace and love me despite the scars I carried. As I mentioned before, it took me a really long time to get over my aborted child's father and the relationship we shared. I couldn't understand why I couldn't move on for so long, no matter how much I wanted to. Later on in my story, I would learn I was holding onto that relationship because he was the last connection to my aborted child. I was desperately trying to hold onto my child, so it felt nearly impossible to let go of Matthew even after he moved away and left no hope of us being reunited.

Despite the struggle to move forward, I did want to be married. Although many post-abortive women can't see themselves having children, I wanted more than anything to be a mommy and have a family. I knew these two things were always in my DNA.

God had those dreams and plans for me. Someone very special was waiting who would become my husband and father of my children. Craig was worth the wait through seasons of loneliness and hopelessness.

It was late summer of 2002, three years after the abortion, when my life changed for the better and I saw true hope for the first time in my life. Craig and I had been childhood friends but hadn't seen each other in a decade. That summer of 2002, our families reunited on a fun day at Cedar Point, "America's Rollercoaster." I had no idea what that day would bring.

Craig hadn't changed much, looking just as cute as ever like when we were kids playing and swimming at his grandparents' house. He still had his bleach blonde hair and striking blue eyes that you could get lost in.

While trying to make awkward small talk in line waiting for rides, Craig was mentally taking notes. He remembered my news of transferring to a new job soon, and, in particular, when my last day would be at the local grocery store in his small town about fifteen minutes from my house. A spark was lit that day between us that set the course for the rest of our lives.

I had to pick up extra hours cashiering and developing film when there weren't enough hours in the floral department. Those were the good old days before we had smartphones, when everyone still used cameras and film.

My shift was almost done on my last day of work in the photo lab at the grocery store. I was pleasantly surprised when Craig popped in to say hi while he was picking up something quick at the store. He continued into the store for his purchase after a quick, "Hello! How are you doing?"

I thought, *Well, that was nice of him to stop and say hi.*

What I didn't know was that, as he left in his car, he was mustering up the courage to come back and ask me out on a date. He later told me if he hadn't turned his car around and gone back to the store that day, he would never have had the courage to ask me out. We were two kids in our early 20s, both with butterflies in our bellies for each other, thinking and hoping we would be imperfectly perfect for one another.

A few minutes after he left, Craig unexpectedly popped back in and asked me if I wanted to go to the county fair that weekend. In complete shock, I started to get that giddy feeling and the butterflies started fluttering again. It had been a long time since I had this feeling over a guy.

Craig really didn't know much about me since we were kids. He certainly had no idea about my dark past. Yet maybe, just maybe, he saw something in me that I didn't see in myself that was worth pursuing.

After that first date at the fair, I knew it wouldn't be our last. Life was becoming amazing with Craig. Quickly I could see there was something different about him. He very well could be the man I might spend the rest of my life with. However, I still wasn't whole and healthy. Deep inside, I was still struggling with my past. The eating disorder was still hidden but overtaking my mind and body. I wanted to be healthy and not to be controlled by the eating disorder anymore, but I was so scared to have Craig know that side of me. Just the thought of sharing how many times I binged and purged had me feeling like such a disgusting person, inside and out.

It wasn't just the eating disorder I was afraid of sharing. I knew at some point I would have to share everything that was ugly about me—my mistakes, failures, sin. The messed-up person I once was and still was struggling to be free from. It would only be a matter of time before he would be curious and ask about the scars on my body left from the accident.

What would he think of me?

Would he want to deal with all this baggage I carried?

Would I be able to share everything with him, even my darkest wound and regret, the abortion?

IT WAS ALL OR NOTHING.

The gift of something unique and special I saw inside of his heart helped me have the courage to share everything. A few months into our relationship was the time I felt safe with him and shared. Craig was my turning point to get healthy. A huge burden was lifted to have everything out in the open, but his reaction would be the crucial turning point to show me if this guy was built to handle everything I carried.

His reaction was nothing short of sincere compassion toward me, ending with an embrace of acceptance. The tenderness of his touch reassured me he didn't want me to battle this on my own. He wasn't going anywhere. He was ready to stand by my side and help me conquer the eating disorder. In that moment of committing to help me through that current struggle, he had no idea of the huge commitment that was ahead for him with the aftermath of my past.

Craig never saw or treated me differently. From that moment on, he was my rock. God knew this was the man whose heart He designed to not only handle but *EMBRACE* a deep healing journey that was already paved for me years down the road. Craig would become not only my safe place to fall but would encourage me when days got hard and trials came. Along the way, he always believed in me to finish God's work that was planted inside.

In the beginning of our relationship while we dated was when our journey with God also started to blossom together. We attended a few classes, learning where we could grow in our church and serve. Serving in the children's ministry was a good fit for both of us, leading us to teach a small group together. This ministry is where Craig and I served for years to come.

After we got engaged, I started to slip back into the eating disorder. I knew if I didn't get professional help this time, the eating disorder would take over my life again. Not wanting to screw up this relationship—like everything else in my life—or the chance to have children, I acted quickly, checking into an eating disorder clinic for a month.

In group sessions, we talked about experiences that contributed to the eating disorder. But one thing was not talked about—the dark secret within me that wasn't to be discussed. My deepest wound and heartache, I carried inside.

Through the years, I taught myself to bury it, yet it was a big cause of my internal pain and problems. I think I even convinced myself that losing my child to abortion wasn't important enough to talk about. That sounds terrible and was actually the complete opposite to what I felt and grieved. However, your mind fills with lies when you stuff trauma in a box and lock it up, never to be opened again. I thought I did a good job trying to erase it from my mind. I literally forced myself to forget about that day, this child, pushing it deep down into the hidden places in my heart.

Still, there would always be reminders (triggers) that forced me to fight my hardest to hold back the heavy tears welling up in my eyes. At times, fighting the tears of suppressed pain was so intense that a painful lump would form in my throat. These instances usually occurred in church around election time when the subject of abortion was talked about. I was that secretly post-abortive woman in the congregation who was hurting inside when no one around me knew what I was carrying. It took every fiber in my body to hold myself together and not shed a tear. That one tear would betray my secret. People would know what I had done. So that tear could not fall! Through the years, the scars of remembrance piled one on top of another until it formed a callus around my heart that would not allow me to grieve.

Jeremiah 29:11

"For I know the plans that I have for you,' declares the Lord, 'plans for welfare and not for calamity to give you a future and a hope.'"

Craig and I got married on a crisp, beautiful fall day in October of 2005. Our life as husband and wife was just beginning, but we would be faced with unexpected challenges just like every marriage experiences. About six months into newlywed bliss that following spring, I got a phone call that no wife wants to get. Craig was hit by a car right in his driver's side door while heading to work.

After assessing him and running tests, the doctors said he had a good prognosis and was very lucky that day. He had a dislocated shoulder and did need to wear a neck brace for a month. Other

ASHLEE MINCER | 49

than the cuts and scrapes, along with a surgery down the road for a bone graph on his shoulder, he healed well with few complications.

Similar to my car accident, the enemy could have taken Craig out that day in an instant, but God wasn't going to let that happen. Our story as husband and wife was just beginning. Craig was in the waiting for me, set apart (Jeremiah 1:5) for the true healing God had for me, the journey He had for both of us. God knew Craig's heart deeply. He created him uniquely with qualities of a strong selfless love and compassion for my healing that was to come. Our days were already written together, and God prevailed, overriding the enemy's destructive plans once again.

Isaiah 54:17

"No weapon that is formed against you will prosper."

Craig's car accident put our plans for starting a family on hold. We already had been in the planning process of depleting my body of the arthritis medication. It needed to be out of my system for about ten to twelve weeks before it was safe to conceive. We felt spring was the time to stop the medication, since the better weather in the spring and summer would make it easier to endure any complications or flare-ups I might have.

> I was that secretly post-abortive woman in the congregation who was hurting inside when no one around me knew what I was carrying.

At the time, I wasn't affected too much by fears of going off of my medication. When I have something in my heart, I go after it with all I have. The experiences of trauma I endured and coming from death to life put tenacity in my soul to never give up on my dreams, never give up when the going gets tough.

I learned through loss and trauma how to endure wars raging around me, both mentally and physically. Living with a debilitating disease at such a young age taught me to be stronger than what I thought I could be, no matter what. No matter the fatigue, flare-ups or loss of motion, I was forced to always keep going. Through everything, I became a pro at blocking circumstances, feelings, and pain. It became a survival mechanism for me. Sometimes it was unhealthy for me, but other times it helped me move forward. During our journey to pregnancy, I suppose I had tunnel vision, simply keeping my eye on the prize you could say.

We became pregnant that summer after Craig was in the clear physically. We were so excited for our first child. I had my first doctor's appointment to confirm the pregnancy, but a few weeks later, unexpected bleeding occurred. Fear swept me into a panic knowing something was wrong when my doctor told me to come straight to her office.

How could this be happening? "God, please let the baby be okay."

Craig couldn't take off work to go with me on such short notice. I felt so alone lying on the table with maternal instinct quickly surfacing. I knew it wasn't good. Then I heard the devastating news, "I am sorry, Ashlee. There is no longer a heartbeat. With the bleeding, you lost the baby early."

No heartbeat... Those words ruminated in my mind over and over again as I struggled to accept the fate I was just dealt.

Driving back home after that appointment, I was numb, devastated, and in tears. I had been hit yet again with a tremendous blow of loss and grief of another child. Alone in my devastation and brokenness, many thoughts raced through my mind.

Could this have been because of the abortion?

Was this partly my fault?

These questions are common for post-abortive women to ask themselves when they have a miscarriage after an abortion. Even if we have become believers, truly knowing better, we can still feel that we are being punished for our sin. However, the truth secretly lies deep within ourselves that we should be punishing ourselves for what we had done.

Sometimes physical complications after abortion, such as damage to the cervix, may result in subsequent cervical incompetence, premature delivery, and complications of labor. So it's easy for our minds to think that our actions have contributed to the miscarriage, or to blame ourselves for possible complications in our next pregnancies.

God certainly does not want us to feel this way or punish ourselves in this manner. The painstaking truth is that forgiving ourselves is the hardest thing to do, to the point that it almost feels impossible. Even if we can accept God's forgiveness because we know He paid the ultimate price, we often still struggle to forgive ourselves.

Romans 8:1

"Therefore there is now no condemnation for those who are in Christ Jesus."

Christmas 2006, we announced the exciting news that we were expecting again. Of course, there was some fear and uncertainty of what might arise during this pregnancy, but it didn't stop our excitement to start our family. We stayed strong and hopeful. God blessed us with our rainbow baby, Lily Grace, on August

28, 2007, a day after her daddy's birthday.

The day she was born into the world, I could never have imagined how my life would change from the gifts God has bestowed to her. I never imagined the amazing miracle that was placed inside of her spirit before she was even conceived for my healing. Our Creator who is omnipresent is even bigger than we could ever imagine.

Our family was just starting out, making memories in a cute little trailer in a nice trailer park. The "neighborhood" was fairly quiet and low key. We fixed it up and decorated to our liking, making it our very own. It wasn't much to most, but we didn't need a whole lot at the time and it fit in our budget.

We were starting to make memories as a family with our sweet little girl. Then things surprisingly changed when Lily was three months old. I was pregnant! We hadn't planned this pregnancy. But we were grateful and blessed for this life that God did plan. This pregnancy was in the safe zone, since I had not restarted my arthritis medication while I was still breastfeeding Lily.

Although we did have room in our trailer to raise two children, we didn't want to stay there forever. A place our children could call home and grow up in was always our goal, without having to pay a lot fee every month. It would get old pretty quickly to always follow the park's rules and regulations. We certainly didn't want to continue paying a pet fee every month just to have our dog live in our own place with us.

Country life was something we both wanted. The new adventure started by looking for land in the town we were already in, Craig's hometown. The best choice at the time, again considering our budget, was to have a premade manufactured home placed on land. We discovered a great deal on one that had been on display just a state away in Indiana. I say just a state away with sarcasm because it was very nerve-racking envisioning our home split in two, traveling for miles and miles over hills, curves, twists, and turns. Anything could happen to create a complete disaster.

After much anticipation and nervousness, our two-piece home was delivered safely onto our land, ready to be set and rolled on the foundation. A specific room in this home from Indiana would become a place where I would find myself on my knees in desperate surrender, where God's glory would pierce the earth. Heaven would come down in my deepest, darkest despair and cover me with God's mercy and grace in that room.

All of the headaches from paperwork, appointments, and hiccups in the process, along with the pregnancy hormones to boot, were all worth it. One month before our son Landon was born, we were all moved into our new home, with the children's rooms painted and decorated. In between the craziness of moving and preparing for Landon's birth, we were able to slow down at least for a day to enjoy celebrating Lily's first birthday in our very first home.

Sept 8, 2008, Landon was born healthy at 8 lbs. 4 oz. by a scheduled cesarean section with no complications. He was such a happy, bubbly baby, never missing a beat hitting milestones. Life was very busy with two children under 2!

The first fifteen months of home videos were like they should be. Sweet moments filled with first steps, first words, belly laughs that you want to bottle forever along with having fun playing and learning with his big sister. Then something started to change in Landon. He started to regress at 15 months and by 18 months we knew something serious had happened to our little boy.

Now home videos consisted of Landon not responding to his name, unable to play with toys appropriately, and no longer being socially engaged. A switch had turned off, dimming the light in his eyes. He was no longer the child who grew and developed like the first 15 months of his life.

The worry, anxiety, and stress we felt only continued to heighten as he began banging his head in frustration from not being able to communicate with us. Words can't explain how hard it is to watch your child struggle like this, unable to communicate their wants and needs or their pain and discomfort. He could not even communicate simple things like telling us his ear or stomach hurt. His intense frustration spilled out in the form of banging his head on walls or the floor, throwing objects, biting, and inflicting physical harm on himself, us, and Lily.

The physical, emotional, and mental stress of this "new normal" was completely exhausting. We were emotionally and mentally depleted and drained. We were left exhausted from the never-ending meltdowns, sleepless nights, and, the greatest hardship, the unknown for Landon's future.

Our marriage was seriously tested and stretched very thin. The unexpected painful trials we were facing started to disintegrate our relationship, marriage, and family unit. We came to a point where we questioned whether we had anything left to give in our marriage. Unfortunately, we both thought of separating and divorce was mentioned more than once in heated arguments.

After nine months of testing, at the age of 2, Landon was diagnosed with autism. Although we knew this was most likely what we were facing, hearing it confirmed was still very devastating. The doctor who diagnosed him said she couldn't tell us where he would be on the spectrum later in life. There was fear of the unknown in that moment, uncertain of the quality of life our son would have.

Craig and I did work through our marriage problems. We came to a point of realizing our kids needed us together more than ever. Through the anxiety, stress, tears, and arguments, we learned how to be a team, not only for our kids but for one another.

I had always wanted to have a third child, but that dream didn't look like it could be reality with everything we had been through with Landon. Even so, I couldn't quite face making a final decision that we were finished having children yet.

Craig and I never imagined that there was, in fact, a beautiful baby already planned for us, hidden in the waiting. This baby would not only be a big piece in Landon's life and development but also would push more hidden healing to the surface for me.

Chapter 5 – The Beginning of the Road

When Lily was a baby and I was pregnant with Landon, Craig and I went through a spiritual drought. Church wasn't consistent. Serving and staying connected within our church family started to diminish.

Craig was working a second job every weekend at a recycling company to provide while I was busy being a young mom and pregnant. It was hard for me to tote a baby to church by myself while also carrying one in my belly, so when Craig was working I didn't go often. Many weeks I couldn't go because of the morning sickness, and the thought of making the thirty-minute drive over the Bay Bridge in the winter seemed overwhelming.

Sometimes these seasons occur in our lives as believers. In fact, I think it happens to all of us at some point in our spiritual journey. We get off track. It's certainly not something we are proud of. We can easily get sucked in the trap of busyness and letting priorities that shouldn't come before God lead us away. For us, it was only a matter of time before we saw and felt the magnitude of what was missing in our lives.

The spirit of God in our marriage was slowly dying out with no spiritual nourishment for our hearts and souls. Life had taken over. This season in the desert taught us where we didn't want to be in the future. Life was not the same when God was not first in our lives and marriage. True fulfillment, peace, and growth are missing.

Lily and Landon were toddlers when we made a transition to a new church a little closer to home. It was a hard decision to leave behind the church where we had served together, married, and dedicated Lily and Landon to God. We had made many friends and connections there, but we knew deep down we needed a change to be able to stay connected and continue to grow spiritually.

Many times, an ending is simply a new beginning. A groomsman in our wedding pointed us to a church he and his family attended. After going to one service, we knew this was the church we were to be at.

I never imagined that this church would be a place where God would peel back the bandage to expose the wound I had closed in my heart and carried for so long.

God saw the big picture for our lives—individually, as a couple, and as a family unit. He will always continue to show and challenge us with things to pursue in order to keep growing, staying connected to Him in the vine.

In the fall of 2014, God had a very specific Bible study planned for me. We had been going to our new church for five years at this point, yet I had never participated in a study. I admit, that is a really long time not to get into a Bible study at your church. Being an introvert had a lot to do with that. Despite how long it took for me to step out of my comfort zone, it was all in God's divine timing. What I felt was a shortcoming was ultimately a divine setup. In our weakness, He is made strong.

I experienced many times through my post-abortive healing journey that my timing was not God's. He loves us so deeply that He will never fail to guide us to the people we need to meet and places we need to step into. Sometimes we might feel like we are not taking enough steps forward or are even falling back completely. But what we consider failures, God sees as an opportunity for a divine turnaround.

> Many times, an ending is simply a new beginning.

Starting my first study, I was nervous yet excited to see what I could learn as well as to enjoy fellowship with other sisters in Christ. I went with a good friend so that helped ease the uncomfortable feeling inside my introverted self.

My dear sister in Christ, Anna, would be the one God chose to first hear my story. She was the one friend who would be by my side from the very beginning until the end when my healing came full circle. She was always willing to listen, check in, and show me with action that she was a part of my support team on this journey.

Anna and I originally connected serving in the children's ministry and bonded further when we discovered both Lily and Anna's son struggled with dyslexia. She had no idea the journey she would be on with me. God handpicked her, knowing she would be everything I would need in a true friend for what He was about to break open in my world. Anna became my supporter, a shoulder to cry on, and the friend I could trust to share a part of my life that I never talked about.

The study was Lysa TerKeurst's *What Happens When Women Say Yes to God*. The night everything changed for me, we had watched a video of Lysa sharing her heartbreaking story. I could relate to how she referred to herself as a "throw-away person." I too felt that way many times in my life, areas where I always felt less than. Then, in a split-second, one specific word she spoke abruptly changed the course of this study for me.

ABORTION

Envision God holding a hammer in one mighty hand and a chisel in the other. BAM! As I heard the word "abortion," the hammer met the top of the chisel and cracked open the scar formed over my heart and soul.

I felt that chisel hit my heart. An intense tidal wave of shock and immense fear swept over my mind, filling every fiber of my body. God was taking me to a place I did not want to go. This was an unfamiliar place that I hadn't been to outside of the abortion clinic. Immediately, I connected to Lysa with this experience from our pasts. It's an experience that only one who has gone through it can completely understand.

I had already shed tears listening to her story before her abortion, but now I was literally holding back the floodgates. Two things crossed my mind simultaneously: without a doubt, the Holy Spirit had placed me in this study, and I wanted to leave and not come back. I almost couldn't keep up with processing what had sprung open. A deep well of emotions started running high and quickly.

That evening, the message was that we all have a *story*, a *history*, and that our history is ultimately "His story." Lysa shared that God's goal isn't to make us comfortable. That truth was evident, as I was feeling pretty uncomfortable and completely vulnerable. His goal, she explained, is to make us comfort-able—able to take the comfort that we have received and give it to others.

After the video, we were asked to go around and share our stories at our small tables. I was as stunned as a deer in headlights. I thought, "I can share some things, but I can't share everything." I had been silent for fifteen years at this point.

Was I even allowed to talk about this shameful secret?

How could I possibly talk about this now?

I knew right away that I would either wither and keep this tucked away in its safe place, or I would embrace this nudge from God. A yes or no predicament was placed right in front of me. I hesitated. Would I close a door or open one?

Women don't usually talk about "it," their abortion. Lysa was the first woman I ever heard openly talked about her experience. God uses people, us, to break through for others in bondage. When she shared this part of her life in that moment, I didn't feel alone like I had for the last fifteen years. Just hearing from one person helped me feel that I wasn't walking this journey alone. A light turned on that there are others like me who have been silent and hurting. Our silence doesn't mean it never happened.

I was the last one at our table to share my story. I knew this was something God wanted me to talk about, and this study was the divine and safe place to open up about such a vulnerable piece of my life. Even so, being surrounded by Christian women, the weight of shame from this unthinkable sin was still there. Even after hearing Lysa be so brave sharing her experience, I still couldn't possibly think of putting myself out there as "that woman." Fear gripped tight as I worried what these women might think of me. Deep down, my better judgment knew they would be compassionate.

That evening, I shed the first tears of brokenness as I surrendered to God and allowed the most painful part of my past out for the first time. This was the first YES of many that I would say to God along the journey. Lysa was the pivotal person who ignited the spark to my healing. I sat unknowingly buckled in with the bar down, about to take off on a ride that would change my life forever.

I left that evening feeling totally exposed with the fear that now others knew this about me, but also with a sense of hope that I could start to open the wound that had been bandaged and hidden for so long.

As Anna and I walked out together after the study, our eyes met. Anna knew I needed the love of Jesus after what I shared. As she wrapped her arms around me, pulling me in tight, her soft voice entered my ear straight to my soul, "You are important and you are loved." I will never forget that moment in time. Her sincere empathy and compassion made me know quickly that she was a sister in Christ I could trust. It was exactly what I needed in that moment to walk confidently out of church.

As I exited through the front doors, I felt a little different than when I came in. A part of my life had been cracked open and a small light of hope began to slowly appear.

After pushing through the rest of this intense first study, Anna and I jumped into another one. The first evening, there was a guest speaker from a local pregnancy center. Here came that hammer again. It tapped the chisel a second time. BAM! The crack was made bigger for more healing to surface. I thought, almost in disbelief, *Are you serious? What are you doing, God? Wasn't the last study enough for me?* The last study was far from enough.

God knows us better than we even know ourselves. He is our Creator and knows the very number of hairs on our head (Matthew 10:30). Only God could see through the deep layers of lies I convinced myself to bury this pain under, never wanting it to be exposed. He could see the layers of guilt, shame, and gut-wrenching, unspoken grief that just kept piling on top of one another through the years. My Savior could see the weight of my brokenness that He didn't want me to carry anymore.

The undeniable truth about my worth in Christ Jesus was starting to open my eyes to a deeper love He had for me. Just like the woman at the well, God was teaching and leading me to drink from the water of life where I would never doubt or thirst again.

John 4:14

"But whoever drinks of the water that I will give him shall never thirst; but the water that I will give him will become in him well of water springing up to eternal life."

The nameless woman at the well recorded in the book of John was an outcast to her people. She was a Samaritan, a group of people utterly despised by the Jews. She was also marked as immoral, having had five husbands and living with a man who was not her husband. She went to the well at the hottest point of the day to avoid ridicule from her fellow townspeople to get a pitcher of water. She had left the well with so much more when Jesus met her asking for a drink. There Jesus makes the woman understand that she needs to confess her sins and change her life by obtaining the water of life.

Although the Samaritan woman was trying to hide her desolation, brokenness, and feeling that she had no value, she ultimately had no control over staying hidden from Jesus and His great compassion and love for her. Just like the woman at the well was desperate for true living water, I too was searching to find and receive that to wash away my self-doubt, past failures, and sin.

Walking through these two Bible studies felt parallel to the story of Jesus and the woman at the well. As Jesus met her in her need, so too my Heavenly Father was reaching down to meet me in my hidden need to be set free. I couldn't see what the healing journey looked like nor the years of hard work that were still yet ahead of me. It was going be a long road, but His mighty and faithful hand would guide me every step of the way until I came out victorious.

FORGIVEN AND SET FREE

As I sat almost in disbelief in the second study, the director talked about what services their pregnancy center offered, including post-abortive healing classes. I had never heard of such a thing or that something like this was even offered to women. For years I thought abortion wasn't to be talked about, let alone something I could heal from. God placed me yet again in a spot of complete vulnerability. Other than my friend Anna, these were mostly all different women in this study than the last. Even though I openly shared during the first study in a small confined space with a half dozen women, I didn't want anyone else to know this about me. I felt most safe and secure when I could retreat and keep this in a box, tightly sealed.

Despite my fear, I knew I needed to be brave and step out of my comfort zone to talk with the director, Mia, after class. Doing so was difficult because I knew others would see me, as well as the tears I wouldn't be able to contain. As hard as it was, this was another soft nudge from God. I kept feeling a push to be obedient to where He was leading me. It was clear I could benefit from the post-abortive healing classes, yet at the same time, I couldn't imagine actually doing them.

Another divine appointment had been set up connecting me to someone that I could confide in to possibly help me work through the guilt and regret deep within my soul. Never skipping a beat, Anna was not far from me, showing her support, as I introduced myself to Mia. I tried to find my voice without totally losing it. Fighting back tears and a large painful lump in my throat, I forced out the painful words that I had an abortion. Right away, without hesitation, Mia opened her arms to embrace me with a deep, compassionate hug, whispering in my ear, "You are forgiven." After talking a few minutes, she wrote my name and number down to reach me about their next post-abortive healing classes that would take place.

These two Bible studies were just the beginning of releasing many tears that I had suppressed for so many years.

The same evening that I met Mia, a movie called *Meant to Be* was recommended, involving abortion and adoption. Craig and I watched it not long after I heard about it. It completely gripped me when it showed through pictures what the aborted boy's life would have been. The life that was taken from this young man included his graduation and wedding day. Falling apart, I ran to the bathroom, sobbing in deep sorrow over my piece that had been missing from me.

Craig rushed to my side, wrapping his arms around me as I fell to the floor overcome with emotion. Words and tears just kept coming out like a flood as if they were the first conversation at a counseling appointment—like the first initial meeting when you spill the beans on everything going on in your life that got you to this point. So were the words of my heartache that I never got to express or work through for fifteen long years.

"I didn't want to do it back then," I sobbed with shameful regret.

"I will never know my child. My child was lost forever that day. I will always regret it. I wish I could take it back." My hyperventilating cry burst forth, not letting up. I couldn't catch my breath. The pain that surfaced was so heavy, dark, and overwhelming.

Moments like this occurred a lot throughout the journey. Abortion as well as the healing and restoration that need to be walked through both cut deep.

Soon after the second study, I attended a Women of Faith simulcast at church with a small group of my friends. Tears streamed down my face, along with mascara that I wiped away as I tried to compose myself. Once again, tears flowed like a flood as I cried out for healing. The message that night was another touch from God, pulling me close to Him, never letting me stay distant anymore with this particular area of my life. My steps were being ordered one at a time.

Here it was again. A third time the hammer tapped the top of the chisel. BAM! I felt the chisel hit my heart again. But more than anything, I felt God's love piercing through my heart as a direct invitation to let Him in. I felt His embrace around me. I just needed to surrender. I needed to surrender completely to Him, despite the fear of the unknown.

That evening, one of the speakers said that to have ownership and grow in the Lord, we must be an active participant in our faith, saying YES to Him. We need to be faithful to our pain, but we can't stay in the cemetery of our past. This was the final place and defining moment when I knew without a doubt God was wooing me to surrender and talk to Him.

Even after becoming a Christian and knowing that God sent His son Jesus Christ to die on the cross for my sins—even my abortion—I could never confess and talk to Him about it. My flesh was unable to let my guard of shame down to be able to open up to the One who could bear the weight of everything I carried.

My Savior was the One who so desperately wanted the chains of my past broken to set me free from the torment of self-condemnation. He wanted to help me work through this unresolved area of my life to be set free and able to soar victoriously into His kingdom purposes for my life.

That following Monday after the women's conference was the

day I said YES to talk to God about my abortion. It was time to totally surrender the weight of deep guilt, shame, and regret I held inside for so long. My Heavenly Father's patience with me was immeasurable over the fifteen years since that day at the abortion clinic. I knew He had been patiently and eagerly waiting to have this special moment with me. He wants more than anything for us to spend time in His presence.

At the time, I was homeschooling Lily and Landon. God was the One who led me to homeschooling. It was not something I chose for myself or my children. Even though I felt a bit unqualified to venture into this new place, people were sent in my path to help me along the way—confirmation that I was hearing the correct path for that season. Homeschooling ultimately was an intricate piece to the plan in order to get me where I needed to be down the road.

I always looked forward to starting my day with God, reading my Bible and journaling. It felt like a luxury not needing to rush the morning with homeschooling. While the kids were still in their pajamas watching TV, I snuck away into my son Landon's room to be with my Creator.

KLOVE was playing softly on my phone as I fell to my knees in prayer. Pretty quickly, the emotions started to build up to the surface, getting more intense the more I talked to Him. Tears streamed as I poured my past out to Him, confessing my sins, until something inside suddenly shifted. An overwhelming heartsick cry burst forth over my past, the abortion, my suicide attempts, and, a longing greater than anything I felt, my child in heaven. The pain and grief for my child were opening up like cracks in a dam as the tears broke through like a flood. My guard came down, allowing the wound to open up and bleed viciously around me.

Some things need to be cracked open and exposed for the healing to happen. An infection will not go away on its own. God wants us to trust Him that He will drain the infection from the wound we carry no matter how long it takes. We can trust God will perform the perfect surgery for our wounds that have left us broken in ways we feel are beyond repair.

The deep grief I felt inside as I talked about my child in heaven was as if I was at the funeral for my baby. There was never a memorial or funeral, no final resting place where I could go to grieve. My baby was tragically discarded and left in another state.

I felt like I was in another place as my face was planted down, resting in arms of despair on Landon's bed. That place was where all my deep-hidden and intricate senses surrendered, allowing the wound in my heart and soul to begin healing. The bed was just a piece of furniture, yet it became a gravesite where my heartache overflowed. Held captive within the darkness of grief, I was envisioning and feeling the funeral in motion.

My baby deserved so much more than what happened on that tragic day. I desperately wished I could take it back. Wished I could have been stronger to say no. A mother's number one responsibility to her child is to protect them especially when the child cannot protect themselves. I let my little one down in the most devastating way.

The more I talked with God, the more I felt peace within. The more I pushed through the barriers was when I could feel God's great love showering over me along with the true freedom through His shed blood.

One specific thing I do remember saying was I was so sorry for what I had done and what happened to my baby. I cried out that I didn't even know if I had a boy or a girl. A hidden deep yearning and longing I carried over the years was now voiced. "I am so, so sorry. Lord, forgive me."

I will never forget a specific song that was playing. Every time I hear this song to this day it brings me back to that moment in Landon's room as a reminder of God's great love in my mess.

Every word felt directly sent to me from my Heavenly Daddy. A huge hug came down and wrapped around me through the words of the song. There was no doubt in my mind that my maker was there in my pain and sorrow. The song playing was "Who Am I" by Casting Crowns.

Ephesians 2:8-9

"For by grace you have been saved through faith; and that not of yourselves, it is the gift of God; not as a result of works, so that no one may boast."

My Savior heard every word, felt every emotion, and collected every tear. As I picked myself up off the floor, wiping away tears and collecting myself to go on with the day, the heavy burden I had carried for so long was starting to lift off my shoulders and my heart.

> Some things need to be cracked open and exposed for the healing to happen.

God can handle our mess. There is no better place to spill our frustrations, pain, hurt, and anger than in the arms of Jesus. He can handle all of it. Jesus bore the weight and pain on His body so we can be free from the darkness of this world and the bondages that the enemy wants us to believe will always be a part of us. God was already in the process of working this trauma out for good. When He turned the tables with bringing me to this place of surrender, the healing didn't happen instantaneously. I still had to continue to walk through the pain of trauma. Memories carry pain and trauma over and over again like a broken record. This healing journey wasn't as simple as being on my knees in prayer crying out to God. It would continue to be a long process filled with hills and valleys, seasons of stillness and seasons of hard work.

Chapter 6 – On Earth as it is in Heaven

Isaiah 65:24

"It will also come to pass that before they call, I will answer; and while they are still speaking, I will hear."

The very next morning after I surrendered and prayed to God, Lily, who was 7 at the time, came skipping in our room before Craig had to get up for work. She plopped herself in between us in bed holding her pink Nintendo DS and asked, "Who is this?"

Nothing could have prepared me for the miracle that was about to be shown to me.

I never thought that God would use a Nintendo game device to perform a supernatural event. But He did, just as he used mud to heal the blind man and fed 5,000 with just five loaves of bread and two fish. Nothing could have prepared me for what God had planned from the very beginning that only He knew of. God speaks to the generations, and He was going to speak loud and clear in the age of game systems.

Our children took selfies and pictures of our cat and dog with this Nintendo DS. Sharks and fish from our trip to the aquarium were on there as well. But this specific picture stood out. This photo didn't quite fit in with the others. At first, we were completely puzzled because we had never seen this person before. We had no idea who this boy was, but we immediately could tell the picture was taken in Landon's room. The hanging seaweed craft I made stood out in the background in the corner of the room. "Naturally," we couldn't figure out who this boy was and why he was in our house.

As Craig got up to get ready for work, I was still intensely studying this picture. The date on the picture showed it was taken on my birthday, April 20, 2013(taken nineteen months before Lily brought it to me). Then the very specific and personal details of this photo came together all at once. Slowly turning, looking into Landon's room, I was almost in disbelief. A flashback came and I saw myself on my knees 24 hours prior in that room.

I looked back down at the photo in awe and wonder. My birth date intertwined with the undeniable appearance of this boy looking so much like my aborted baby's father, Matthew, was the moment I was instantly touched by God.

Words almost can't explain what I felt in this moment in time. The blindfold made of the enemy's lies that had been wrapped tightly around my eyes for so long slowly fell to the floor. I felt His great love for me come down from heaven, embracing me.

In that moment I heard a silent whisper, "I was with you, my beloved. I heard you cry out to me." The sweet delicate sound of the Holy Spirit that lives inside whispered softly to my heart again, "This is your boy, Ashlee. I loved you then. I love you now. I will always love you." I did not hear the audible voice of God, but His words given through the Holy Spirit were loud and clear, deep in my heart and soul.

I was hit in an instant with certainty that this was my son. When a mother carries her baby for nine months, she has to wait for the moment of delivery to actually see her child face to face. The moment we hear our child's first cry and physically see their face is when we know without a doubt this is our child we created and carried for nine long months. That's what it felt like for me. The boy I was looking at was my son who I carried for a short period of time.

Heaven came down to earth that day. I was so overwhelmed

with this miracle that was given to me. Time stood still as I sat in awe of my son's beauty and perfection. That day, I couldn't stop crying and kissing the image of his face, telling him I loved him so much and wanting to be close to him.

Not only did he look just like his father, but I could see myself in him along with traits from my dad's side of the family. I was completely undone. There was a miracle gift from the heavens resting in my hands. Only God!

Job 5:9

"Who does great and unsearchable things, wonders without number."

Jesus's free gift of salvation was the very reason why the picture was taken on my birthday. God was reminding me that I am reborn through His Son, Jesus Christ. He was showing me that He knows me personally, including the day I was born into this world. Earth has no sorrow that heaven can't heal.

My son was 13 years old in the picture, and I named him Miracle that day. There is more to the picture that would later be revealed in upcoming seasons when I was ready. I still didn't know all of the continued steps and seasons of His healing for me. It was going to be a slow process of discovery as the layers would slowly be pulled back in the years to come.

Journal Entry 11/11/2014

"My baby boy is so beautiful. His purpose is to let his light shine, God's light. The glory of God's kingdom is in this picture. All glory to God."

Our prayers are powerful, allowing heaven to invade earth. Miracles are a result of God's supernatural power that transcends the laws of nature for His purpose. They are personal and always happen in response to a human need. Miracles are confirmations of who God is that interrupt the natural cause of events with precise timing to bring GLORY to God. If we keep our focus on our Heavenly Father, He can weave miracles into the most mundane day.

We don't have to work for miracles or strive for demonstrations of the Spirit. Rather, by *FAITH* we walk in the knowledge of being sons and daughters who have an inheritance now to show forth the glories of God. He takes His Spirit residing in us and activates that power for His glory.

He demonstrates His grace without warning. On our softened and prepared heart, He will spring forth with this grace. Not by might nor by power but by His Spirit.

Luke 15:7

"I tell you that in the same way, there will be more joy in heaven over one sinner who repents than over ninety-nine righteous persons who need no repentance."

Sometimes we fail to realize that we can have an amazing encounter with God, even supernatural, yet still have some things to work out. After receiving this miracle, I was convinced I had worked through the entire healing process. I had reached the point of surrender, falling on

> Our prayers are powerful, allowing heaven to invade earth.

my knees to repentance and emptying my heart of what I thought was everything in me that needed to be released. However, like I said before, God knew this road would be a long one even if I didn't. Years of deep hidden pain still needed to be tended to.

Only God could know exactly what I had been through in my life. I hid my immense brokenness under a well-kept appearance of happy wife and mother. For so many years, I covered my regret so well that I didn't even really know what I needed or if I needed healing at all. There were many pieces to the healing that needed to come to pass, especially the most difficult part—forgiving myself.

It's not in God's nature to reveal all of His plans for us at once. We grow closer to Him when He reveals things in layers and seasons, at a slow pace to the rhythm of His heart and timing. He longs for that time with us more than anything. Time with Him is when He shows us how we can have a true intimate relationship with Him, communing with the Holy Spirit daily. Through the seasons, He wants us to remain teachable to show us time and time again that He is who He says He is. Our Creator is the One who is in control of our lives and knows what is best for us.

There is a backstory on this pink Nintendo that the Holy Spirit used. We actually never bought it. Craig's mom worked at Lowe's, and it had been left there. There were pictures of the previous owner, a little girl with blonde hair. Time passed and no one came to claim it, so she gave it to Lily.

Craig deleted all of the pictures from the previous owner, and then there was a period of about ten months that it must have been lost in our house because the kids didn't use it for quite a while. Those ten months of no usage were revealed through the dates on the stream of pictures. Plus, we had forgotten the kids even had it.

It wasn't until the day I landed on my knees that Lily started to use the DS again, taking selfies of herself and our cat Milo. Amazingly, Lily had used the DS after Miracle's photo was taken, but she never discovered it until God's perfect timing.

What is even more amazing is that there were about 19 months from the time Miracle's picture was taken until the day my precious Lily delivered it to me. That was a long, precise delay and timing led by the Holy Spirit to reveal it just a day after I cried out to God. Everything was orchestrated by God behind the scenes with everyone in our family unaware of what was taking place in the spiritual realm. The details are truly amazing and continue to leave us in awe and wonder of how great our God is.

Seeing Miracle's and Lily's pictures side by side on the Nintendo DS shows the visual connection between brother and sister that these two shared. No distance between heaven and earth could sever that bond.

On the DS, there are three icons you can choose to mark your photo: a three-leaf clover, a heart, or a star. The icon on Miracle's picture was the three-leaf clover, and Lily's was a heart. While we associate the three-leaf clover with luck, it was originally used by St. Patrick to represent the Holy Trinity: Father, Son, and Holy Spirit. One leaf, yet three parts; one God in three Persons. The heart on Lily's symbolized to me God's heart and His strong love for her. She was chosen for a greater purpose beyond this earth.

God had gifted Lily at a young age when she didn't even know it. Nor did she truly understand the Holy Spirit who lives within her. She was chosen to play a miraculous role in God's story, and I hold tight to it with praise for all that God has done for me and blesses me with.

A month after receiving my miracle picture, I had a profound dream. When I woke, I knew without a doubt it was something God would lead me to. I was standing on a stage in front of many women. Some were young teenagers, and some were older. They represented the post-abortive. I knew, at some point in my life, I would be led to share my testimony.

My dream then switched to portraits of beautiful, precious faces of children, infants to preschool-age, black and white sketches of the unborn in heaven. They were sketches of children that He created for unique plans and purposes to fulfill here on earth but who never got their chance. I understood quickly that I would be a vessel, a voice for the unborn and post-abortive women who needed tremendous healing from their pasts. These vivid dreams would often come to the forefront of my mind through as a powerful reminder of His assignment over my life.

Chapter 7 –
Stepping-Stones

With many experiences in life, there is usually a process we need to go through to eventually get to the destination. There are hops, skips, and jumps in the journey. You could find the perfect shape and smoothness in a stone to skip on top of water, meticulously aiming for the direction you wish to throw it. But no matter how much effort or skill we put into the throw, it will still go in uncertain directions. There is always a possibility of that stone landing in the opposite direction that you thought it might go. It was the same with the scenario with our manufactured home being split in two to be moved miles to our land in the country. A swift wind could have landed us in a completely unexpected situation.

This is what our life can feel like when we trust God through the process. He turns our course unexpectedly, leading us to places we never thought we would go and to meet people we never imagined meeting. These crossroads are scary to step into when we look at them from our human perspective. In fact, many times they are not ones we would choose for ourselves. On the flip side, the Holy Spirit does not give into fear or uncertainty. This is where unshakable FAITH makes its entrance and is tested.

Inner transformation grows and blossoms through the process. There is beauty in the furnace of the unknown. We need to remember the pressure and pain are causing something of great value to rise. God takes His time in His navigation system for our lives, but He always keeps His word. He's forever faithful. If we get off course, we don't need to jump ahead and panic. We will be repositioned back to His alignment for our lives.

FIRST STEPPING-STONE: Homeschooling

For a long period, I was in awe of what God had done, displaying His presence in my life. You might call it a "heavenly high."

We had a family vacation planned to Wisconsin Dells soon after I received Miracle's picture. The first evening at the resort, I snuck away for some quiet time on the bed with my journal, pen, and the Nintendo DS. As I spent time in God's presence, I couldn't shake the feeling I got from the Holy Spirit that my God was up to something. There was something about His demonstration of love for me in my mess along with seeing my aborted son was wrapped in glory that made me know, without a doubt, this wasn't meant to be kept in a box.

> Inner transformation grows and blossoms through the process.

I didn't know what it was or how His plan was going to look. I *did* know for certain that what had been done so far was more than anything I could ever imagine. It would take patience and promptings in His leading through the next years to see the book that was already written come full circle (Romans 8:28).

Journal Entry 11/21/2014

"The story of Miracle is not over. It is just unfolding. His story was not meant to be kept silenced. My son Miracle was created for something more than anyone could imagine. He is a testimony of God's love, mercy, and grace. Miracle is God's light to God's kingdom in eternity. I pray for the timing I share this story, my story, My God, God's miracle. I have a lump in my throat holding back tears. This is so precious to me. My story is about healing. It tells who God truly is. It can help others heal from their pasts. God, You would not perform a miracle with my picture for it to be kept in a box and closed. Jesus, I love You and want to come to You empty-handed and offer my life in complete surrender."

The vacation we took was a much-needed break from the reality and struggles with homeschooling both kids. It was one of the YESES I agreed to during the first Bible study. I tried everything I could to accommodate both Lily and Landon's unique needs with dyslexia and autism. I printed out Lego and Angry Bird worksheets for Landon. I was applying professional techniques for dyslexia, desperately trying anything and everything to make our days fun while learning. Nothing seemed to help, and I eventually felt I was failing my kids by keeping them out of public school.

Without a doubt, I knew God told me to pursue homeschooling, but it was looking nothing like I thought it should. Many times, I was just thankful we got through the day with an ounce of progress and accomplishment. It clearly looked and felt like homeschooling was a mistake, but in God's eyes, it was the perfect stepping-stone to the next destination.

This first stepping-stone felt slippery, unsteady to the point I felt I was about to fall off at any moment. But God's plans are solid foundations no matter how rough the storms are that we face.

God sent me a dream at a pivotal time when I was struggling

with self-doubt and quite honestly doubting His plan. Through this dream, I was reminded to trust His leading no matter what the cost and to never doubt my faith that I have in Him!

The Dream

Confident and empowered, I was walking on water. Then I started to sink slowly. Each time I started sinking, I looked to the heavens, focused on my Savior. As I did, I started to rise and continue to walk on water until I reached land. He gave me this dream to remind me of the story of Peter doubting God, how his faith diminished when the wind and turbulent storm came.

Matthew 14:28-33

"Peter said to Him, 'Lord, if it is You, command me to come to You on the water.' And He said, 'Come!' And Peter got out of the boat, and walked on the water and came toward Jesus. But seeing the wind, he became frightened, and beginning to sink, he cried out, 'Lord, save me!' Immediately Jesus stretched out His hand and took hold of him, and said to him, 'You of little faith, why did you doubt?' When they got into the boat, the wind stopped. And those who were in the boat worshiped Him, saying, 'You are certainly God's Son!'"

Faith is more than a word. It's an action. It's trusting God's stepping-stones that lead us one by one into the next chapter. He wants our faith planted and rooted deep in the soil, strong and unwavering in order to step out on uncharted waters.

James 2:17

"Even so faith, if it has no works, is dead, being by itself."

Most want to stay in the boat where it's safe. For some, it's too frightening to even take the step into the boat. They think staying on the shoreline away from any possibility of being blown by the wind and waves is the safest place to stay. Faith is trusting that He will not allow us to sink when we feel we are drowning. Faith takes confident conviction that God will do what He promised. I knew He was going to see me through homeschooling even when I couldn't see how.

SECOND STEPPING-STONE: Autism School

I would say Landon was the most difficult to homeschool. Both of my children need structure and routine in their days. Achieving this in a home setting just didn't seem possible. About halfway through the school year, Landon fractured his wrist in two different places after jumping off the couch for sensory input. After a visit to the ER, he was referred to an orthopedic doctor where a cast would be put on for at least four to six weeks.

As we met the doctor, we informed him about Landon's special needs. We explained that he might not understand, be scared, and need more time to process everything. The doctor totally understood as his son is on the spectrum as well. It was such a blessing in disguise to find a doctor who understood special needs kids. The subject of homeschooling came up, and I confided how it was not working out as well as I thought it would. He mentioned an autism school that his son attended about 40 minutes from where we currently lived. Ironically, we knew of this school and had even gone for a tour when it was at a different location when Landon was much younger. At that time, he was too young to even be able to attend, but we were researching all of our options for his future when he was first diagnosed.

> Faith is more than a word. It's an action.

With meeting this doctor and the commonality we shared, I felt a pull from God redirecting us to a better place for Landon than homeschooling. My faith was stirring that the autism school was a stepping-stone to Landon's future. Behind the scenes, it was in fact a divine stepping-stone for me personally. I stand amazed how God can use something that seems as insignificant as a fractured bone and turn it into such a blessing in the process. He can use anything for good in our lives.

By the time of Landon's follow-up to get his cast off, we had obtained the Ohio Autism Scholarship for him and was making so many positive gains at his new school. We knew this was where he needed to be. However, transportation was not available from our area to the school. Some schools did transport students to the autism school, but it was not a guarantee they would provide that. It all depended on being under a certain amount of miles, and the ultimate deciding factor was the school district itself.

While I continued homeschooling Lily, Craig would drive Landon to school before work and then Lily and I would pick him up after. It wouldn't be long before the 30-minute commute to and from would start to wear on us. We knew for the long term this wasn't feasible yet held on by faith.

THIRD STEPPING-STONE: The Move

In our dilemma with transportation to and from Landon's school, we decided to make a decision that seemed pretty drastic at the time. We really never second-guessed in the beginning, because we were focused on Landon's future for the long haul not just in the moment.

We decided to put our house up for sale to move closer to the school in order to try and get him transportation. We looked in a town that already transported to Landon's school. It was a guarantee that if we moved there, we wouldn't have to drive him. But as we looked at houses in that town, it didn't feel like home for us. We just couldn't see ourselves there.

After seeking God's direction and praying, we came to the decision to move to my hometown on the lake with determination to try and push for transportation.

Not long after we put our house on the market, a couple expressed interest and wanted to buy it. However, length of time at a new employment for the buyer put the process on hold. That was the only thing stopping the sale. We were frustrated but trusted this was where God was leading our family. So, we decided to rent out our house to the couple until the sale could be finalized.

We had been looking at houses and found one that a friend's family member was thinking of possibly selling. It was a much smaller home than our last, and we thought at the time we wanted to downsize. The house was right across the street from the city park, which seemed like a perfect place to be. However, this plan fell through as the owner decided he was not ready to sell. That was a blessing in disguise. At that time, we didn't think we would have any more children in the future, and we would have been pretty cramped with a third child in that house. God knew what He was doing amongst the bumps in the road.

We jumped ahead of God, finding another home we really liked. In a knee jerk decision, we were very close to putting an offer in only to be brought back to reality. We couldn't when the financing for the couple wanting to buy our house was on hold. God had a plan and everything set in place despite these obstacles we kept running into.

Since we did not sell our house right away, we were obviously not in a place to buy. My dad had been renting out my childhood home that I lived in since I was 12. After my parents' divorce, he stayed at the house until he transferred to another state for his job. He let us know that if we needed a place to stay, we were more than welcome there. He would just need to let his tenant know to have time to find a place and move out.

To our utter amazement, the tenant was planning on informing him that she was actually moving out, into her childhood home that she inherited. This wasn't coincidence. This was a bold confirmation that we were exactly where God wanted us.

Unexpected directions lead us to greater levels of faith where we will see nothing is impossible with God. The stepping-stones up to this point were building our faith not only to keep following God's nudges of change but to trust as well. Pushing through the uneasy feelings of uncertainty allowed the little miracles to weave in and through the transitions.

As we conquered each stepping-stone, our doubt in God's plan started to fade. He was teaching us not to abandon the promises He has given, especially when things weren't working out the way we thought they should or in our time. He will always make a way when there seems to be no way. Our intimacy with Jesus is our greatest weapon. God calls us outside of our comfort zones to live in a place of total dependence on Him.

Through the stepping-stones, I was praying for a new beginning for Landon as well for our family. God was answering those prayers. However, I had no idea of the love story that was being rewritten behind the scenes over my life. This new beginning involved God bringing me back to the place where everything happened. The home where I experienced the aftermath from the abortion along with healing from the trauma from the car accident. The home I returned to from both physical and emotional traumas to heal and move on with life. Yet, true complete healing never occurred back then. I left that home to marry Craig looking like a person who was all put together, who had everything going well for her. On the outside, my physical wounds left visible scars but healed. The scars that cut deeper on the inside never did.

Chapter 8 –
Building Faith

Process is the place where faith can build. The process is the pliable place where we allow the Potter (God) to make a masterpiece out of the clay (us). Certainly the "stepping-stones" were very uncertain at times for us. We questioned many times if we were making the right decisions along the way, especially when challenges came and direct answers were not at our fingertips.

We knew our God is so much bigger than anything we come against. He was truly in control of everything in our lives, even if that meant we had to wait on answers. We could have given up the stepping-stone to sell the house when the process wasn't as smooth as we wanted. We could have taken that as a sign we shouldn't continue or maybe it wasn't the right plan. Many would have.

Holding onto God's nudges and confirmations is critical, along with remembering He is forever faithful. His promises are forever and true. Otherwise we will fall back into thinking our way is better because it "feels" more secure. We take God out of the front seat, placing Him in the back as we take over the wheel to our lives and destiny. Suddenly "Jesus take the wheel," our favorite lyrics to sing when things go awry, vanishes from the forefront of our minds.

In the beginning of putting our country house up for sale, the sun peaked through the light spring rain forming a perfect rainbow over the house. Craig took an amazing shot of it. The promise hung over the house where heaven pierced the room where God heard my cry. It was a beautiful sign to remind us to trust in His plan. Where He leads us, He will always provide a way. We held onto that perfect arch of promise despite the difficult circumstances, trusting the house would sell. It didn't happen in our timing, but it did in God's. Faith was building when we surrendered, allowing painful stretching to occur in order to continue to be teachable.

> Process is the place where faith can build.

Soon after we moved into my childhood home, the school year started back up again. Landon returned to the autism school, and I was going to continue to homeschool Lily. This was our plan, what we thought God wanted for us until things started to quickly unravel soon after they began. I found myself questioning God again. *Why was all this happening? Why did He lead us to make this big move for it to come to this? This wasn't the plan.*

We found out that Landon could not get transportation at the same time that I was overwhelmed with not having Lily's curriculum ready. Then, unexpectedly, Lily voiced she wanted to go back to school with friends. Several dilemmas crossed my mind. It was overwhelming to think that if I put Lily back in public school the kids would have two different schedules with two different school districts and a 30-minute distance between. We were not sure how we were going to manage not only transporting Landon everyday but the cost in mileage to do so. In the whirlwind of plans turning totally upside-down, my faith and trust were fading.

In the end, Lily and Landon both went back to public school in my hometown where I grew up.

In the moment, I didn't understand God's plan, but that didn't mean He didn't have one. Homeschooling and the autism school were simply stepping-stones to get me back home where continued healing would occur. The connecting of the dots didn't register to me right away. In the meantime, our family was still enjoying the change along with making memories in the town and home where I had so many memories.

Healing can be instantaneous, or it may take years. Our part is to trust in God fully, praising Him through the storm, giving thanks for the restoration that has begun. When it's a process, sometimes it is because our thinking can't handle the change and all that God has in store. It's too big for us in the moment so He slowly unravels hidden answers for us. The process teaches us how to enter the corridors of heaven where we are to live and dwell. We learn to cooperate with the plans of heaven and not the things in the earthly realm.

The kids loved living where I grew up, and especially residing in a neighborhood with other kids to play with. It was just the opposite of country life. Our country home was private and peaceful, with plenty of yard space surrounded by fields of farming, but we had also been secluded.

Lily and Landon were both thriving at the new school, making new friends. Landon's teacher and aide from kindergarten had even transferred to his new school, so he had familiar faces to help him get acquainted and ease into a new environment.

God truly had everything set up and in place. In hindsight, moving into town was something Landon needed in his development. It was a critical learning milestone for him to have more opportunities to be social, playing with kids as well as learning the dangers and boundaries of living in town on busy streets.

Going back to public school also helped Landon build his socialization to the fullest. Many children at the autism school couldn't communicate like Landon was able to. It took us time to see what God was doing in Landon's life when ultimately the autism school was only meant to be for a very short season. I learned to be grateful for the stepping-stone—even the slippery, uncertain ones.

Before we moved from the country back to my hometown, I had written my first book about my story out of obedience. It wasn't easy for me, and I didn't have a vision for it. I just knew I had this miracle of God's glory He wanted me to share with others. That was a given. I didn't know at the time that the story was still unwinding and would take another four years to unfold completely. I eventually put away that first book and let it collect dust, but as the years came and went, God was persistent with the call to *write*.

> Healing can be instantaneous, or it may take years.

As the years progressed and I saw more of what God was working in my life, I knew the book needed to be rewritten. For quite a while, I didn't write, still confused of what or even how to write. There were many times I wanted to quit. The enemy was attacking in many different areas in my life. It seemed when I would start to type again, another hit would come like clockwork.

When God tells us to pursue something specific by giving us a word or promise many times, it's not necessarily for that exact season we are in. It can be, but many times it's for the next season or even years down the road. God wants time with us in between the call until the promise is fulfilled. This is the place where we hear from God intimately in our relationship. Dwelling in His presence is where we allow Him to comfort us, teach us, guide us, mold us, and build us up to be equipped to handle the promise in the time it's to be given.

When you know deep within what God has called you to do, you can't just quit when the going gets tough. Jesus calls us to obedience in order to transform ourselves to be more and more like Him. Obedience comes out of love for our Father. If we quit, then we are saying no to Him. It will always leave us with regret. Obedience demonstrates our faith in Him and is also an act of worship.

Romans 1:5

"Through whom we have received grace and apostleship to bring about the obedience of faith among all the Gentiles for His name's sake."

When you fall seven times, you get back up eight. Staying on the ground is never an option. The journey of writing encompassed many falls and defeats. I had always told God if this book were to come to completion, it would ultimately be His, His words, His wisdom and vision. I lost count of how many times I continued to surrender this to Him, prayed and sought for discernment for His revelation to write over those four years.

The falls and defeats came through writer's block and fear from the enemy that I would never be able to write. I felt unqualified. During these years, God was still writing my story. I simply needed to be patient in the process to walk through it to the other side. Writing would come again at the right time. The journey in writing was also building faith, believing what God already believed in me.

Journal Entry October 2017

Dear God,

I have been distant, distant from You, distant from prayer. I hear You still calling me to my destiny and purpose. I may not know the full picture, God, but I continue to surrender it all to You. I can't do anything without You. Lord, I am sorry for my shortcomings, my sin. Help me to move forward. Help me to see Your vision. Lord, I ask for wisdom in this season and the next.

Lord, I surrender......

In Jesus's Name, Amen

In the few months after we moved, I received an unexpected voicemail from a Mia, who asked me to call her back. I was confused who this Mia was. Come to find out, it was the director from Heartbeat Hope Medical. To be honest, I forgot what her name was after that night I met her at church a year prior.

When you fall seven times, you get back up eight.

I was caught off guard when I called her back to find out why she was calling. She was informing me about their post-abortive healing classes that were coming up. My mind was in a standstill not knowing what to say as I thought about Miracle's picture and the book I wrote.

I thought, *Surely, I'm fine. I don't need these classes.* I shared with her the miracle God gave me and that I actually wrote a book. I politely declined, thinking I had worked through everything. I was fine.

God knew that wasn't so. That was the very reason He had placed Mia into my path when He did. At this moment in time, I said no to receiving extra help in healing only to realize I would be in desperate need of it down the road.

Mia was interested in reading the book. I was a little nervous what she might think of it. My confidence in writing was not very high back then. Her response helped me to continue to push through.

"What an amazing journey you have been on. This is a beautiful story of His redemption!! I would love to see the picture! Please keep going with this. I believe God is going to use this in a mighty way."
~ Mia

Those two words never left me: "Keep going…"

The time came when the couple could finally finish the process and close on buying our house. What a relief! We finally made it. God is good! We look back with thankfulness for the hardships and His timing of waiting. We could see how He was building something within us that we couldn't do on our own. Our faith in Him was stretched stronger through the hard road of the uncertain, trusting in Him alone.

One huge milestone was out of the way and now we could focus on buying my childhood home. Just like we experienced with selling our house, the process is never an easy one. There will always be hoops to jump through when selling or buying a home.

In this next waiting season to buy my dad's house, God gave me peace. Just like the rainbow arching over our house in the country showing His promise that sale would eventually be complete, I knew everything was going to work out.

I attended a "Women's Night Out" at church. The theme was houses and home improvement. Coloring sheets of different houses with the same scripture on them were placed on the tables, along with paint color swatches from a home improvement store with scriptures as well.

Hebrews 3:4

"For every house is built by someone, but the builder of all things is God."

I almost couldn't believe what I was seeing. This gathering was so fitting for the season I was in. The coloring sheet right in front of me was identical to my childhood home. Every corner, the unique swoop in the roof above the front door, down to the detail of the two apple trees was on point except we had two crabapple trees. Just smaller apples!

Oh, those crabapple trees that my dad planted. God knew I had a love-hate relationship with those trees when we moved here.

The crabapple trees are the most beautiful through the seasons. In the spring, white flowers burst forth and blossom. In the fall, the leaves slowly turn to their amber shades. In the winter, the bright red crabapples that are left, withstanding the climate change, standout as the brilliant white snow nestles in between.

I love witnessing the trees' metamorphosis through the year, but on the other hand, they are always shedding something. The broom always seems to be in my hand sweeping the deck and sidewalk. Whether it is piles of leaves, piles of white flowers, or piles of red crab apples, I am always busy sweeping.

God has a sense of humor, and I know He enjoyed speaking to me through these trees with a smile on His face. Besides the humor, the seasons of these trees remind me of seasons in my life. Seasons where I needed to grow, be still, and seasons of pruning.

Mesmerized by the coloring sheet, I knew I was definitely taking it home to frame. I could already see it finished before I started. With excitement, I placed it in my folder to take home anxious to add the color that would bring life to the page in this chapter that God had brought me to.

There, after I colored the house light blue, was my home, complete with trees that made the signature touch. I knew this page was designed and sent to me that night by the hands of the Holy Spirit, whispering God's promises of hope back into my heart again. What God starts, He completes.

I had no idea what God was continuing to build on this journey. In fact, I thought the journey was over after finally purchasing my childhood home. We closed on the house one day before our anniversary. What an amazing gift that the delay was over as we finalized with signatures at the title office. From the time we put our house in the country up for sale until we closed on purchasing my childhood home, it had been about 17 months. That's many months of patience and faith-building.

We followed the promptings of the Holy Spirit even though things didn't turn out the way we wanted or thought they should. God is good in the waiting. His waiting serves a purpose for reasons we might not even know. When it was time for closing, the interest rate went down. There was another blessing tucked inside the long waiting of obedience.

The sweet aroma of nostalgia swept every corner and room in this house as we were making our own memories, painting, and decorating as our own. In standstill moments, I caught myself off-guard daydreaming of the past while sitting on Lily's bed and gazing out the window. Reflecting on my life, joyful tears would fall along with thankfulness and praise for God's goodness.

Only God could so perfectly orchestrate building the bridge to new beginnings here. The room where I was once deep in darkness, wanting to leave this earth, now had new life. Watching Lily do arts and crafts, listen to music, and enjoy decorating her room brought me back to the young Ashlee who once occupied that room. I could see how everything was coming full circle in so many amazing ways.

Psalm 34:18

"The Lord is near to the brokenhearted and saves those who are crushed in spirit."

One day I was looking for old photographs of Craig and me from our time dating. I was in the basement looking through a few bins of pictures old and new. Some pictures were at this house growing up. Others were from the years Craig and I dated, wedding photos, as well as pictures of Lily and Landon when they were younger. In the shuffled mix, I came across a photo of myself that I clearly remembered.

IT WAS THE DAY OF THE AORTION

I was in my blue and white striped swimming suit lying in a lounge chair on the deck by the pool in Florida. My eyes were closed, trying to block out the trauma, searching for solace.

I had seen this picture before a few times through the years and always remembered it. However, that day I was instantly drawn to the date in the bottom corner in red. The date was 6/27/99. I never remembered the exact date of the abortion. I just knew that it had taken place in the beginning of the summer.

An intense urge came over me to find Miracle's picture to look at the time it had been taken. The numbers 6 and 27 looked so familiar. With eagerness, I raced up the stairs to the first floor and swung around the corner, continuing to run up the flight of stairs to my room on the second floor to find his picture. As my eyes saw the numbers, I was completely undone with tears streaming down my face, overwhelmed at how great God has been in the details of my healing. The date and time matched!!

God only knows what we experience and how we are truly affected, because He is the One who never leaves us. When I felt completely alone, drowning in despair at the abortion clinic, He never left me. His love never left. His grace never left. His mercy never left. He was telling me this in this moment of discovery. I had always wondered if the time meant anything and here was proof that it truly did. This hidden treasure was to wait to be revealed until God brought me back home.

Only God can perform a miracle in healing so private and personal, showing Himself in ways so powerful and unique in our lives even when we don't feel Him beside us. He was there with me that tragic day, holding me up at the same time my son ascended to heaven to be in Jesus's arms of love and care. I was wrecked once again with how great and mighty His mercy and love for me is as each piece slowly unraveled.

Chapter 9 –
Healing Within
New Life

During spring vacation in 2016 while soaking in the pool at the resort in Virginia, Craig started a conversation that took me by surprise. Suddenly, I had so much excitement bubbling up inside. The thought that we could possibly have a third child filled my heart with complete joy.

I could never imagine what another precious beautiful life would bring to our family. This baby's first year of life brought out unexpected grief in areas I was unaware needed to be worked through.

Not long after vacation, we started the planning process to get pregnant again. First, I needed to make an appointment with my rheumatologist to discuss stopping the shots I took every week. After twelve weeks, my body would be in the clear from all traces of the medication in my system, and I could safely take prednisone for flare-ups when I needed to.

This pregnancy was a little different from my others. For one, I was older and we didn't get pregnant right away. There were many days my joints were really affected once my body was totally depleted of the medication that it depended on. Sometimes I was in tears with pain, stiffness, and utter frustration, barely able to get in and out of the bath on my own in attempts to loosen my joints. I didn't have a choice but to push through the pain and struggle. I just kept praying the next month just might be the month of a positive pregnancy test.

Luckily, pregnancy often puts women like me into remission when they become pregnant due to the high levels of hormones present in the body. I was fortunate that was my experience while pregnant with Lily and Landon. My body never felt better than when I was pregnant, actually.

The day before Christmas in 2016, we got a positive pregnancy test. What a Christmas present that was for us and our family that year! A new adventure was just in the works, another new beginning and a new miracle of life growing.

A day before Valentine's Day, I had my 12-week ultrasound. I was so excited to have the first ultrasound and see our little baby for the first time. Craig had planned to take time off when we found out the gender later, so he didn't come to this ultrasound. This appointment was very different in the sense of conversation that took place. The topic that was brought up usually does not take place at an ultrasound, nor was it really appropriate.

My OBGYN who delivered Lily and Landon always had a sense of humor, and not always the best bedside manner. You either liked him or you didn't. His sense of humor never really bothered me as it was never offensive. I just understood that was his personality.

The day of the ultrasound, God was speaking to me through my doctor. His words spoke truth from God's heart, even though it was a huge and painful trigger for me.

My doctor must not have reviewed my medical history to remember that along with my two pregnancies, I also had a miscarriage and an abortion. If he knew I had an abortion, I know he would have never said what he did as it was obviously a sensitive subject for me and very awkward for him.

Since I was just 12 weeks along, the ultrasound needed to be vaginal. As the instrument was placed in for the ultrasound, the doctor was showing me the baby on the screen. His voice was filled with excitement and wonder, pointing out the baby's body parts moving with the strong visible heartbeat. There was a miracle of life growing. Who wouldn't get excited about that?

Psalm 139:13

"For You formed my inward parts; You wove me in my mother's womb."

"Do you see as I move the instrument closer to the baby, it senses it and moves away?" the doctor asked me.

"The baby doesn't want this instrument in its space. It's foreign to the baby. I have never done an abortion. I don't know how doctors can. That baby feels something in its space. Its instinct wants to move away from it. Can you imagine an instrument sucking that baby out?"

I was almost in shock of what he just said. *Did he really just say all of this?*

Seeing the baby on the screen and then hearing that was surreal. I was in absolute awe of seeing my little baby moving all around and yet painfully triggered to the day of my abortion, grimacing inside and trying to digest what my aborted baby experienced.

God was not punishing me with those words from the doctor. He was allowing me to grieve what happened to my baby while at the same time proclaiming truth and justice through the doctor's words.

The doctor spoke of the horrific truth and injustice that is done to the unborn during an abortion—the truth of what babies experience in the womb during the procedure. Truth isn't always easy to hear, but it is necessary for justice to prevail. God wants voices to rise up to end the murder of His children who were created for a purpose, who are fearfully and wonderfully made.

As I watched my little peanut move around in my belly, I heard God's encouraging Spirit say, "Ashlee, be My voice of truth and justice. Be a voice for your son and the unborn. Be a voice for the women and men who have been hurting like you. I have brought you to this place. Stay with Me. Will you continue to say yes as an empty vessel, to fill the shoes of one soldier in My army to stand in the gap against abortion?"

It was then I remembered the dream I had a month after I got my picture of my son. That dream of standing in front of a podium on stage, looking out at many women in the audience, was obviously foretelling that I would be sharing my story publicly one day. I also remembered those two words from Mia after she read my first book: "Keep going."

The words from my doctor were not meant to be a condemning trigger by my Heavenly Father. It was a reminder of what He had done so far in my story and what He had for me in the future. He wanted me to stay strong and true to where He was leading me. Only He knew when it would occur. My responsibility was to listen to His voice, be obedient, and surrender to His plan, no matter how hard the road would be. I knew I needed to continue to step out in faith, wherever it would take me.

2 Thessalonians 1:11-12

"To this end also we pray for you always, that our God will count you worthy of your calling, and fulfill every desire for goodness and the work of faith with power, so that the name of our Lord Jesus will be glorified in

you, and you in Him, according to the grace of our God and the Lord Jesus Christ."

I left that appointment with peace and joy for this life growing inside of me. What the doctor said might have knocked my spirit down at first but then turned to confidence stirring within that God would use my story to help others making a difference in the world of abortion. I had peace with that. I didn't need to know all the answers or what was in the future. I had peace

> The doctor spoke of the horrific truth and injustice that is done to the unborn during an abortion.

that God sees me, knows me, and loves me. And that was enough in that moment. It was all I needed to be still, resting in His promises.

We were so excited for this pregnancy that we had names for both a boy and a girl picked out before we knew the gender. Craig had the idea for a girl to be Lucy, named after his late grandmother Lucille. I just loved that name "Lucy." I wanted my late grandmother's name, Patricia, incorporated as well.

We decided on Lucy Patricia for a girl and Christian Edward for a boy. Edward is Craig's and Craig's father's middle name. Craig's father, whose first name was Clarence but who was known to everyone as "Eddie," unexpectedly passed away when I was seven months pregnant.

The big ultrasound day came for the gender reveal. It's a boy!

Christian Edward arrived three weeks early at 8:12 a.m. on August 12, weighing a healthy 8 lbs. 4 oz. and 21 inches long. Besides arriving early, he certainly didn't fit the criteria for a premature baby.

Our family was on cloud nine with the soft, sweet presence of a newborn again after nine years. It was a special moment when we didn't think this day would be reality. Yet this bundle of joy had been in the waiting all along. All the days of our sweet Christian were already written. So many unforgettable memories were being made. Landon was experiencing many firsts with the role of big brother, and both kids just fell in love with the baby. Seeing how Christian has added to our family in so many different ways, we couldn't imagine life without him.

It wouldn't be long until Christian's precious life would start to poke at a very tender spot again, pushing unfinished healing to the surface from the depths of my soul. Triggers were starting to make an entrance again, especially in the winter when Miracle would have been born.

Times that Christian slept on my chest with soft, soothing lullaby music in the background put me in another place— *moments that were erased before they ever had a chance to be.* As I held Christian's tiny hand, I wondered what my first son would have looked like as a baby, wishing I could hold him and cuddle him. What would Miracle have looked like as a newborn, toddler, and small child? What would his first word have been?

Grief was starting to spring up again since that day I landed on my knees crying out to God. Just as any mom who loses a child here on earth grieves, so was I grieving and missing the child I never got the chance to meet. The one significant difference was that I was connected to his death. The guilt and shame of that is pretty incomprehensible—a loss and regret that cuts deeper than the depths of the ocean.

There were so many emotions and steps in healing I had not taken yet and didn't know I needed to face and conquer. I would need help from others to do so. There was a reason God placed Mia in my path a few years before in the beginning of the road.

Time stood still in those days as I embraced my newborn in the same home where I had not had the chance to rock Miracle. With each back and forth motion of the rocking chair, memories drifted in and out. This home was where my life altering circumstances occurred and where the physical healing from those traumas took place.

-   The unwanted abortion.

-   The intentional car accident.

In Christian's first year of life, Miracle would have been 18 years old and graduating high school. I was watching friends I graduated with at their child's last football game, last homecoming, last prom, and planning graduation parties.

Unfolding right before my eyes were celebrations and memories being made that I should have been experiencing at the same time with Miracle but never would.

What sport would Miracle have liked to play? Would he have enjoyed music like Christian, maybe as part of the marching band?

Witnessing my friends celebrate these milestones with their children pulled on my heartstrings. A deep yearning in my soul silently begged for any kind of moment with my son. I had his beautiful face to look at, but I didn't have his physical presence to embrace him with the love I have always had for him. I grazed through life to the place I was now with an amazing husband and family, yet a huge piece was of me was missing forever.

The sweet stillness cuddling Christian in my arms was mixed with joy and thankfulness along with deep grief and pain. A mixture of bittersweet emotions swirled around simultaneously in my soul. I was in awe how God had taken my life full circle to bring me back home and bless me with a baby we never thought we would have. I could see more of the fullness of the plan God had been working on as Christian eagerly scooted in his walker to his favorite room in the house, Lily's room.

As I would gaze out the window in a daze, memories swirled in my head, reminiscing again. I couldn't hold back the tears. I had many moments like this, particularly in Lily's room, as a rush of overwhelming grace and goodness swept through me.

I had been taken from the darkness of death to light, pure joy-filled light that radiated the restoration transpiring in my soul. Where death had plagued me, now new life was blossoming with every pitter-patter of Christian's little feet.

I still wrestled with conflicting thoughts of how I could be at this place. It was like a brutal game of tug-of-war. I should be fine after the miracle and God's goodness already given to me. He had blessed me beyond measure, yet my soul was still totally crushed. I talked myself into thinking I was okay because I was so humbled by the miracle He placed in my story. No matter how much I fought to keep the rope on my side, I couldn't anymore. I was still completely broken, even after all the steps in healing that He brought me through. It was time to let go of the rope and surrender. I needed help.

I wanted to trade mourning for joy, but I was unable to do it on my own. The enemy wanted me to think that I wasn't a "good Christian," allowing guilt to enter my mind. The enemy was working hard to convince me that I should never have been the person chosen for this miracle.

His lies whispered, "Look at you. You are a complete mess after what God did for you. You are not a strong person." I felt I was just as much of a mess in this moment as when I was sitting years before in the Lysa TerKeurst study.

> I wanted to trade mourning for joy, but I was unable to do it on my own.

As I surrendered on my knees again, knowing I couldn't do this anymore, I knew I needed Him more than ever to rescue me. God lovingly taught me that it is okay not to be okay. No matter where God has taken you thus far or the good gifts He bestowed along the journey, it's okay to still need help.

He cares deeply for us through the hills and valleys of the process. There is no picture-perfect timeline in healing or a specific way to heal from trauma. But the One in whose mighty arms you rest through the healing IS perfect. Our sovereign Lord is compassionate and gracious, slow to anger, abounding in love and faithfulness. He upholds us with His righteous right hand.

Genesis 28:15

"Behold, I am with you and will keep you wherever you go, and will bring you back to this land; for I will not leave you until I have done what I have promised you."

Chapter 10 – Samuel: He Has Heard

When I named my son Miracle, it seemed perfect for that time, in that moment. Something that helped with my grief was to hear other women's stories on YouTube. There was a connection through our loss and brokenness. I didn't feel alone hearing their stories.

I then came upon a few stories where God revealed to them if they had a boy or girl, and even their child's name. I thought, *I wonder what Miracle's name really is?* Certainly he has a God-given name. There is a scripture that was telling me my Heavenly Daddy could and would reveal if I asked and believed.

Matthew 7:7

"Ask, and it will be given to you; seek, and you will find; knock, and it will be opened to you."

So I prayed and asked God to reveal my son's name in His way, in His timing. The first name I heard in a story after I asked was "Sam." The name hit me. Samuel. I remembered that I had Samuel written in my journals many times through the years and in different ways. As I scrolled through the pages, I came across so many "Samuels" along with a word that was given with miracle linked to the name. The light bulb turned on. I realized God had been telling me along the way. It just hadn't clicked for me. He was waiting for me to "seek and find" when the time was right. My big confirmation was when I looked up the meaning of Samuel.

Samuel
"God has heard."

As instant tears flooded my eyes, I felt God's presence reminding me, "I heard you cry out to Me, my child." Every word was heard. Every painful tear was felt. It's amazing how much God loves us and has for us when we seek Him intimately through the Holy Spirit.

I knew God had revealed a significant connection between my son Samuel and Samuel in the Bible. I needed to spend more time with Father God to see what exactly He wanted to speak to me. My Samuel in heaven carried a similar anointing but not identical—different and unique, hence the name. God would unravel His wisdom slowly as I sought Him to understand better.

Samuel in the Bible was set apart before he was even conceived. Before his birth, he was a chosen man for God. His mother, Hannah, prayed for God to give her a child and in return she promised to give him to the Lord. She cried out to Him for a child, and He remembered her and gave her a son.

When Samuel was weaned, Hannah presented him to God at Shiloh, in care of Eli, the high priest. Samuel was a prophet who listened to God, anointing the first king of Israel named Saul. As a prophet, he exhorted Israel to turn from idolatry. I truly know and believe God had my son set apart just like Samuel the prophet.

We know from scripture in Jeremiah 1:5 that God knew us before He formed us in the womb. Before we were even created, we were set apart, chosen for His unique heavenly assignments to fulfill. Before we were born, He appointed us to be prophets to the nations. All of our days were ordained for us and written in His book even before we came to be.

God knew that my son would leave this earth soon after he was knit in my womb. Even then, God had a plan in place for my Samuel and me. God appointed my son to be a prophet to the nations about abortion. My precious Samuel is a face of the millions aborted in heaven, declaring and decreeing these children, the unborn, have faces and names. His beautiful face displays God's glory for abortion to be overturned, abolished, and no more.

"I heard you cry out to Me, my child."

My son's spirit is a loud voice from heaven to declare that babies who are aborted are life. They are precious babies from conception with their own unique gifts to offer the world. Samuel was aborted in fear of possible birth defects, but it's been displayed through my son that every life matters. Every life is sacred. Every life is intentional, abounding with dignity and worth to shift the paradigms of this world in a divine way that only they can.

Samuel was set apart as God's mouthpiece for what He wants the world to see, know, and understand when it comes to the horrific act of abortion that has distorted truth, shifting to lies and deception from the enemy.

It was really hard for me to comprehend and accept that his

days were already in place and would be brief. God knew everything that was going to happen and still had a plan to use my loss and pain for a purpose. Samuel's purpose and destiny had already been written

We can see the difficult truth in why God allows suffering to occur. Through pain, He pours out His grace and love. It was Jesus's pain on the cross that brought the miracle blessing of our salvation. It is our pain that can be used for good as His glory shines in and through our lives. Our lives that once were misguided messes filled with sin and misery are now turned into merciful masterpieces.

We can ask so many times in life, "God, why did You let that happen? If You are good, why couldn't You stop this from happening? What I am experiencing is unbearable."

These are questions we hear a lot from others who haven't found Jesus yet. Even believers can catch themselves asking these questions in the most difficult times of tragedy. It's easier for us to ask these questions when we have endured and lost so much. From heaven's perspective, God is always at work in ways we don't see in the moment. Even in our most heart-stopping, crushing moments, He is still our Way-Maker, Miracle-Worker.

He sees the sin that caused the fall of man and the bad things we experience because of the sinful choices we have made in our life or from the consequences of the sins of others. Either way, God sees. God intervenes. God always has a plan.

The way He intervenes and allows the suffering to be experienced does not feel good. Neither does it feel good for Father God to witness our suffering and pain. He is just like parents who will, out of love, allow their children to suffer a little while if it is for their own good in the bigger picture. We call it "tough love."

A car comes barreling down the street as our child, unaware, steps out. We will intervene in a split second, forcibly pushing our child out of the way. The push could cause a bone to break, but a broken bone is better than trauma to the whole body and possibly death. We don't think twice about allowing the pain to occur from that push if it will save them. This doesn't mean it won't pain us to see our child hurt, but to spare their life, that pain is worth it. The pain God allows us to go through can be turned for our good, ultimately drawing us closer to Him.

There are also times God allows suffering not because we have sinned but as a way to display His glory to the earth. The blind man in the book of John is evidence of the miraculous power which God put forth for Jesus to heal him, displaying God's glory.

John 9:3

"Jesus answered, 'It was neither that this man sinned, nor his parents; but it was so that the works of God might be displayed in him.'"

In the seasons of trauma of my past and the longsuffering I endured, all I could see were my terrible choices. I felt the loss and grief buried inside me as I pushed down the shame and guilt of those choices. I couldn't see God in the mess of my life. I didn't feel His presence. Yet, He was there through it all.

A predestined road map was paved that would bring me to a place of true restoration, healing, and freedom. I needed to walk it out no matter how long it would take or how great the heartache I would endure. Once I stepped in, walking through it, I would come out on the other side a whole new person filled with overflowing joy, praise, and thankfulness for the scars. I would not only feel God, but also learn to see Him in and through everything I experienced.

Chapter 11 – Forgiven and Set Free

There was one person able to help me through the deep, unattended scars. I reached out to the person God had placed in my path at the beginning of the road, Mia. She was the person who would understand and help me.

I sent an email expressing I was having a very hard time and finally realized I needed outside help. There was no possible way I could do this on my own anymore. Three years had passed since the time she called me about their healing classes that I had declined over the phone.

Mia responded, "Sometimes God allows those layers to be pulled slowly so we can heal and process in the time that is right, perhaps to nudge us in taking another step in the healing process. We have our post-abortive healing retreat called HEART coming up next month, and there is one spot left. I don't think this is coincidence at all. If you would like this spot, let me know ASAP."

Mia was right about God pulling the layers slowly in the process.

Little whispers led to big nudges at just the right time to take another step in the journey. Meeting Mia that first evening was just the seed being planted. Now was the time for it to be watered through her ministry to be able to grow and blossom into all God has called me to be.

The retreat was for a long weekend. It would be the first time I was away from Christian. I knew God sent His angels on dispatch to save this spot for me. I needed to push through any anxiety and fear to step into this. Without hesitation, Craig said, "Take the spot. We'll figure everything out."

The retreat was completely confidential with women who devote their time and gifts to this incredible ministry. I was reassured that I could sneak away from life, hidden and secure in the presence of women who truly cared for me to solely focus on myself.

I am truly grateful for my husband along this entire journey. Not just anyone can embrace the depth of healing from abortion when the child is not his. Never once did he waiver through the rivers of tears and pain I experienced over and over again.

Soon after I arrived at the retreat, I was led to my bedroom to drop off my suitcase and belongings. My heart skipped a beat when the facilitator went to unlock the door to my room. My hand covered my mouth as I let out a gasp of utter shock and surprise when I saw the name that was assigned to me.

"LILY"

The week before we got to the retreat, the ladies and I were assigned a flower name to be prayed for before we arrived as well as all throughout the retreat. I stood in awe and wonder as I looked at my daughter's name in elegant calligraphy printed on a blue piece of paper. Mesmerized by the sight on my door, I felt God tangibly inside my soul where the Holy Spirit dwells.

Out of all the flowers I could have been named, I was given my daughter's name. My flower child, who God chose and set apart to become a beautiful part of God's miracle story. God was reminding me that even in the intricate, fine details, He is ever-present.

I was starting to let my guard down as I stood in the final resting place for healing, nervous and vulnerable. I felt from my Father that it didn't matter the time or the distance it would take to get me there. He would be faithful to see me through till the end.

Another amazing detail on my door was the room number—room 21. A month after the retreat, Lily started her very first season of soccer. And guess what number she was randomly assigned? You guessed it: 21!

As I walked into my room, I felt a sense of peace and security as I set my suitcase down. Sitting on the wooden desk was a handmade picture of an orange Lily with a scripture written on it.

The orange ink used to make the lily dripped of the Holy Spirit. God speaks through all creation as He is Creator of all things.

Job 12:9-10

"Who among all these does not know that the hand of the Lord has done this, in whose hand is the life of every living thing, and the breath of all mankind?"

The Lily could have very well been crafted with any color— white, pink, yellow, or even peach. Yet, a color was purposefully chosen to broadcast the very detail of God's voice and nature.

I had always wondered why Samuel was wearing a bright orange shirt in his picture. The orange stood out against the dark black coat he wore as the outstanding bright light of the Holy Spirit shone upon him. The only thing I could conjure up at the time was maybe orange was Samuel's favorite color. It wasn't until I was at the retreat that God would reveal more of His heavenly mysteries.

In the spirit realm, orange represents the fire of God, deliverance, miracles, and healings. Orange lilies have a very special meaning to me and Lily now. We have an orange lily planted in our back yard, and she has orange silk lilies in a vase in her bedroom as constant reminders of God's mighty personal conversations with us. They are vibrant reminders that even when life hits hard, diminishing the fire within us, God's fire for us never grows dim.

The first line of tears slid down my cheek in that moment as I saw that orange lily picture and heard from my Heavenly Father, "I see you here. I am with you." This beautiful, handcrafted picture was just the first of many special gifts I would receive at the retreat. I wanted to plant myself on the twin bed and just be held by Jesus in His loving arms, letting the tears continue to flow. There was no time for that. I needed to quickly collect myself if I didn't want to be late for dinner.

Many volunteers made delicious, hot meals for us. The love and compassion in the hands that prepared the comfort food was felt through the aroma that pervaded the room. The table settings had different colors and themes for each meal. This ministry was absolutely amazing with so many thoughtful little surprises and delicate details to help us walk through the most painful part of our lives. Mighty, powerful, personal prayers were prayed. Little notes and cards were filled with encouragement, love, and truth from scriptures.

The book we studied was called *Forgiven and Set Free*. Some of the things we worked on were:

- *Where we needed healing*
- *The character of God*
- *Relief and denial*
- *Anger*
- *The need to forgive*
- *Depression*

• *Forgiven and set free as well as acceptance*

We learned about post-abortive syndrome. This was something that I had never heard of until the year before the retreat. I assumed all of my messed-up choices and sin were because I was simply a messed-up person, a failure. I didn't truly understand the depth of the root to my internal pain and problems. I never linked them to the abortion until I saw the worksheet given at the retreat. There were so many I checked that I had experienced through the years. This side of abortion is not talked about or educated from the abortion clinics. No one tells you the emotional and psychological effects it will leave you with for years and decades.

God wants to heal all the detailed parts and invisible pockets of our soul. He is intimately connected to our experiences and how they have affected us. Only God can know the depths of healing for us, deeper than we could ever imagine. He is that good of a Father to us. Blueprints were etched with divine surprises to bring healing and wholeness and in the right time, we will see everything fall into place. The best view comes from the top of the mountain after the hardest climb.

Throughout the retreat, I was mentally exhausted yet at the same time it brought the most joy and freedom as well. I met women there who I could talk with and relate to. It helped me to know I wasn't alone in the pain as we shared our stories together.

The facilitators were nothing short of amazing, abounding with love, compassion, and hearts that truly displayed Jesus through their ministry. God had gifted these women in a special way to help heal the wounded and broken.

The depth of this healing was intense. Sometimes we don't truly know our heart's deepest needs and desires until God separates the waters, reaching down to bring us out of the bondages of brokenness and despair.

Countless times, the tears just kept coming. I wondered at times if they would ever stop. This was the place I didn't need to be ashamed to let them fall. I discovered things about my experience and myself that I never knew. Those things were pulled to the surface to be mended and cut off for good.

One of the hardest things for me was to truly forgive myself. I was doing all this hard work that was helping me be able to move forward, yet one thing still remained, held so tight and deep inside for so many years that I couldn't let it go. I didn't know how to let go and forgive myself.

The retreat was what I needed to allow my heart to surrender the power I didn't have to forgive myself in order to receive the power of God's forgiveness. Most of the women deeply struggled with this as well.

Mia asked, "Do we even have the power to forgive ourselves?" That question stopped me in my tracks. The answer is no. We don't have that power. That's where Jesus stepped in, coming down from the Father of Lights to die for my sins and the scars I couldn't carry on my own. Through the journey of healing, I felt I had the power to forgive myself when, in reality, I couldn't possibly have that strength.

The guards blindfolded Jesus, mockingly taunting Him as each one passed by, spat upon Him, and struck Him in the face, piercing His head with a crown of thorns. Each intense blow scored deep lashes on His holy, sinless body—stripes that bled for all my sin.

He took my pain and guilt from the abortion as He died the most unfathomable way through crucifixion. The blood of Jesus and His body hung on the cross paid the price for my sins. The cross is where He wants us to leave it, for good! When we do that, our bondages break. We are set free from chains within ourselves and all that we carry on our shoulders that we were never meant to.

When I stop and think of the unimaginable horror Jesus went through for me, it puts me back in check of what not to run from but *embrace*. He embraced me and everything I am, good and bad on that cross.

Sometimes we need to step through the hardest tests of healing in order to come to a place of total surrender. He is a patient God who always provides a way out. In the end, ultimately that way out is through Jesus's blood that washes our sin as white as snow.

There was a particular session where we discussed giving names to our children. Women find that naming their baby helps to identify with their loss. A name brings order to the chaos of emotions, gives focus for the grief, and opens the gates for years of unexpressed grief to be released. A name restores dignity to the broken image of the unborn.

As I sat in the circle during a group session, I found myself fighting back thoughts and emotions that I never planned to expose. Emotions linked to the personal details of my son started to rise up inside even as I fought so hard to keep them at bay. The enemy crept in, flooding my mind with intense lies.

> "Do we even have the power to forgive ourselves?"

I never planned to tell any of these women about Samuel. I felt it certainly wasn't the time or place. With all the emotions running high already, now I was trying to hold back the precious miracle that was given to me.

I could feel the tears welling up as my body tensed, not wanting to move in fear that I might not have control over this situation. I tried to convince myself I could hold onto this tight grip to reach the other side silent and unscathed.

"Keep this in, Ashlee. Pull it together. Don't allow this to go there. This is

not the place," I kept replaying in my mind, trying to convince myself I could.

A woman spoke how she heard of women receiving a name for their baby from God, yet she struggled with that. The enemy came in so hard in that moment that I was in fight or flight mode within seconds. Guilt swept over me.

Dark lies invaded, swirling around in my mind, "Look at you. You shouldn't be here. You were already given a name and much more. You don't deserve to be here. These women need healing, not you." Those were the exact words I heard the enemy say. In that moment, I believed him. The tears I held so desperately within couldn't be contained anymore. I didn't want anyone to see me on the verge of a break down. How could I possibly share this miracle given to me when these women were still in the process of healing and naming their babies? The room was caving in, suffocating me. I needed to escape this overwhelming feeling I couldn't bear anymore.

All I had been holding inside started to release like a flood. "I am sorry, excuse me," I said as I bolted like a jet ready for takeoff. The words barely came out as I opened the door and closed it behind me quickly. The fear and anxiety was weighty.

Once I was in the next room alone, I could fully release everything I was trying so hard to hold in. Once the tears spilled out, I finally was able to catch my breath again.

Frustrated with myself, I was thinking, *"Ashlee, what are you doing? Pull it together."* One of the rules was we were to never walk out of a session. I couldn't believe I just did, but in the moment, I couldn't control myself.

How was I supposed to handle this now? Where did I go from here? Immediately, I felt terrible for leaving with no explanation. I knew I needed to pull myself together, dry my eyes, and take a couple deep breathes in and out. It was time to head back in to face this dilemma.

I apologized for walking out, reassuring everyone it wasn't from what anyone had said although I know it appeared that way.

The enemy wants us to go around the same mountain to keep us bound and broken, to allow the lies to override truth and prevent us from taking any steps forward. The Lord wants to do a work in our hearts for major breakthrough and freedom.

John 8:36

"So if the Son makes you free, you will be free indeed."

During the break after that group session I talked with Mia, explaining why I got so emotional and left abruptly. She felt my healing would be hindered if I withheld the miracle God gave me from the group.

The more we talked, the more I could see God's truth again, and the enemy started to flee from my thoughts. I told her that when I was ready and the timing was right, I would share. However, it came down to the last session and I hadn't spoken up. Mia gave me a nudge with a silent look of "it's time to share." She knew there would never be a perfect time and we were getting down to the end of the retreat. Then she spoke up for me in my weakness.

"Ashlee has something she would like to share with the group. I expressed to Ashlee that keeping this in would only hinder her healing."

Letting my guard down, I read what I wrote in my journal to summarize what God had done on my journey. The women were so thankful that I was able to share with them. They were in wonder of God's glory. I truly had nothing to fear in sharing. In that moment, my hope and prayer was that sharing my story would be an encouragement to the others and that God would reveal their babies' names. Seek and you shall find.

Sharing my story at the retreat was part of God preparing me for when the time would come to testify publicly, outside of secure, confidential walls. His preparation was at a slow pace, building strength in order to equip me for the next season, the chapter where God's prophecy would be fulfilled from the dream He gave me of speaking. The divine appointment for that would be surprisingly right around the corner.

The morning of the last day, they held a memorial service for our babies. We were to pick a date for our child's birth certificate. Sitting at my desk, I was pondering one. It was hard to pick a specific one because I would never know Samuel's birthday. The unknown tugged on my heart. What I did know was he would have been born in the month of January or February. I felt a bit silly trying to even guess his birthdate. After wrestling back and forth in frustration, I settled on a random date in January. A few months later, God would reveal that this date was not random at all.

I had also asked Craig that morning if he would like to adopt Samuel as his son. Without hesitation, he said yes. Samuel Miracle Mincer was officially part of our family in writing. He had a place within our family. He always had. I would soon receive something I had lost and never imagined ever having—my lost son's birth certificate.

During the retreat, I had mentioned that Craig and I had a miscarriage before we had Lily. Mia asked me if we ever had a memorial for that baby, which we hadn't. She said they would love to give me the chance to honor and acknowledge that child as well. There were many times through the years that I thought more of my aborted baby than the one lost in the miscarriage. With Samuel, I had a hand in his death that lead to tremendous pain, regret, and shame. My mind understood that the miscarriage was ultimately God bringing that child back home to heaven from natural causes and reasons still unknown.

A few years prior, I asked God if He would tell me if we had a son or daughter in heaven from the miscarriage. I had a vision that we had a girl. The vision was in black and white of a little girl with long hair flowing as she danced around. I said, "God, if this is correct, You need to give me confirmation." I asked Craig if he ever wondered if we had a boy or girl. If so, did he have a feeling about it? I did not share with him what I felt God was telling me. I wanted to hear what he was going to say without prompting. He responded, "A girl." God had more confirmations down the road that we have a daughter in heaven waiting for us. There were specific details about our daughter that would be revealed just as with Samuel.

We were going to have the blessing of having a birth certificate for our daughter as well. As I tried to think of a name, sudden revelation came. I remembered the name we had picked out for if we had a second daughter—"Lucy." God spoke clearly, "Her name is Lucy Patricia. You always had a Lucy Patricia. She is with her great grandmothers in heaven."

There is nothing that compares to the presence of Jesus and the many hidden treasures He has tucked away to surprise us with. He wants to bless us with details that have been missing from our lives. These hidden treasures come at just the right time, allowing us not only to receive a special gift but also to experience personal communion with Him.

Thinking of Lucy's birthday was more difficult than Samuel's because we couldn't remember the exact month we got pregnant or the month we lost her. I called Craig to tell him about our sweet Lucy Patricia who was in heaven with our grandmothers. We were going back and forth, trying to remember, until we finally landed on March. I never chose a specific date for March like I did for Samuel's birthdate. Why, I had no idea until about a year later.

One year after the retreat, I joined a small group of ladies to go and pray at an abortion clinic during the 40 Days for Life. On our drive home, Judy, who drove us that day, mentioned her granddaughter, Lucy. I lit up instantly, telling my friend next to me about the baby Craig and I miscarried and how we ended up naming her along with honoring her at the memorial service at the retreat.

A minute later, Judy said, "Today is Lucy's birthday." Something hit me in my spirit. We were in the month of March, the month printed on Lucy's birth certificate, the birthstone in my necklace with all five of my children's birthstones.

That day, March 26, I knew without a doubt God was revealing my daughter's birthday just as He had with Samuel's. When I got home, I pulled out her certificate. In the blank spot after March, I wrote in 26. That day was Lucy's 13th birthday.

Psalm 139:1-7

"O Lord, You have searched me and known me. You know when I sit down and when I rise up; You understand my thought from afar. You scrutinize my path and my lying down, and are intimately acquainted with all my ways. Even before there is a word on my tongue, Behold, O Lord, You know it all. You have enclosed me behind and before, and laid Your hand upon me. Such knowledge is too wonderful for me; it is too high, I cannot attain to it. Where can I go from Your Spirit? Or where can I flee from Your presence?"

As I continued to keep my spiritual eyes and ears open, more answers were unlocking from heaven to satisfy my heavenly longings and desires of the deepest despair of my heart. Our omnipresent Father wants to fulfill our desires exceedingly and abundantly more than we could ever imagine or dream. Is anything too big for God of the universe?

Back at the retreat, the final day came for the memorial service for our babies. I had no idea what to expect, as you could tell from my simple ponytail, jeans, sweatshirt, and tennis shoes. That's how clueless I was about the experience that would occur. If I would have known, I would have dressed less casually for the occasion.

The visual I had in my mind was being in a circle, talking in remembrance of our children and sharing what we wanted to express to our children. Nothing could have prepared me for the ambiance and beautiful, delicate sight when I walked into that room. It was a place that I desperately longed for. For eighteen long years, I had always wanted true closure. I needed to be able to feel my son at rest after all these years.

The room was beautifully set for a very intimate and personal moment in our healing, the final resting place for our children. I could feel the somber yet uplifting atmosphere the moment I stepped into the room. There was no doubt the Holy Spirit's presence was there that morning. Worship music was playing, and we were each handed a red rose.

I was completely overcome with emotion within one breath. There was a long table spread with white linen and lined with our children's names. The scene represented the funeral for my precious baby boy, the final resting place I never got for my son. This was the exact moment I had felt when I was crying uncontrollably on Landon's bed all those years earlier, grieving for my lost baby.

God had prepared in the waiting a beautiful ceremony to heal my heartsick cry and deepest longing. Samuel Miracle was written on a nametag with a little crown above his name. He was crowned officially, being a child of God for a purpose. A light blue votive candle with a white rose rested on the elegant table setting by his name.

SAMUEL
Language/Cultural/Origin: Hebrew
Inherent Meaning: God Has Heard
Spiritual Connotation: Instructed of God

Scripture: Proverbs 21:3
To practice righteousness and justice is more acceptable
to the Lord than sacrifice.

MIRACLE
Language/Cultural/Origin: Latin
Inherent Meaning: Wonder
Spiritual Connotation: Marvel

Scripture: Psalm 98:1
Sing to the Lord a new song, for he has done marvelous
things; his right hand and his holy arm have
worked for salvation for him.

The same was done for our Lucy Patricia, with a light pink votive candle. The service was closure I needed to truly lay my grief down before Jesus.

The facilitators kneeled on the floor before each of us, taking the time not only to acknowledge our children but to acknowledge each of us personally. A personal letter was created for each of us and read by our facilitator as if from God. As the facilitator read my letter to me, she almost couldn't contain her emotions with tears of empathy dripping from her eyes. I felt so much love and compassion in that moment. I felt from her heart and from my Heavenly Daddy that I truly was a child of God. I was so overcome with the love, care, and compassion these women in this ministry displayed. I wouldn't be where I am without them. God's Spirit spoke to them, whispering truth, comfort, and love into my aching heart.

My dear princess Ashlee,

It brings Me great pleasure to see internal beauty blossom inside of you and to watch you grow up in Me. I delight in every moment we spend together. I delight in giving you the desires of your heart. I delight in hearing you call out to Me. Don't ever feel like you are unimportant to Me. There is no reason for you to feel unsure of My love for you. I am always waiting for you to delight yourself in Me and in My love. It is My pleasure to bless you abundantly. Don't look to anyone else to meet your deepest wants and needs, because you will only end up empty and disappointed. Only I can turn your tears into joy and fill the emptiness in your heart. So delight yourself in Me, and you will live life to the fullest because you are My delight.

Love,

Your King. Your Lord of Eternal Delight.

Psalm 37:23

"The steps of a man are established by the Lord, And He delights in his way."

After lighting Samuel's and Lucy's candles, I laid the white roses inside the basket next to Jesus's picture. With more tears, I said, "I finally lay it down." I accepted my past. I accepted Jesus's free gift of love and forgiveness, but most importantly, I accepted forgiveness for myself. My thoughts were no longer stuck on the past and what was lost. Now I was filled with tremendous joy, knowing that my son was with Jesus, and that God calls me by name. The glorious day will come when I will see both Samuel and Lucy for eternity. What a reunion and celebration that will be!

I was a totally different person coming out of the retreat than I was going in. I am forever grateful for the women who prayed and loved on me unconditionally through that deep healing process. I saved every anonymous note and card addressed to "Lily" that was filled with encouragement, strength, and truth in scriptures and love. I will hold onto those little treasures forever.

It's in the secret place with our Creator that He will set us free. He sees the cracks in the foundations that need to be tended to. We may not even realize some of the cracks that need to be filled. When we face fear, wrong beliefs, hurt, pain, and trauma, we need to remember the One who is our ultimate healer. My Daddy tore open the seal on my heart, eventually leading me to the retreat in order to deal with the root of everything I had experienced and kept hidden.

On the first day of the retreat, we were asked to write down some things that we carried. Along with tremendous guilt and shame, I also carried a deep, heavy wave of grief that consumed me. The grief I carried was unshakable with the sorrow of not just losing my son but losing his entire identity for years. Samuel's identity with who he was created to be was gone, never to be known, as if he didn't matter while life carried on.

My son I never got the chance to meet meant everything to me, but his memory and worth were lost in the silence. So many years of silence had buried my deep grief.

At the end of the memorial service, the facilitators gave us back the paper of things we carried, tucked in an envelope. I held the envelope in my hands, trying to remember what I had written. Ashlee (Lily) had changed. She had been set free. That's why I couldn't remember what I had written. As I opened it and saw what I wrote, I stood amazed at how far God had taken me in just those few days. What I wrote was now gone, erased. It was left at the foot of the cross. Beaming, I declared, "I no longer carry the grief that I came into this weekend with." The promise was to no longer carry this heavy weight. I tangibly felt it lifted off of me, feeling free, floating on true freedom.

> It's in the secret place with our Creator that He will set us free.

God wanted to rewrite the ending chapter of the abortion, making it clear He wasn't going to settle for the damage that had been done. The retreat was the sudden turnaround that was waiting for me to end the chapter of guilt and grief, giving me the capability to forgive myself. It was always planned for the right time and season, even though it took me years (and felt even longer) to reach this place. God's Holy Spirit was the best scriptwriter to end this chapter and move into the next chapter of my life.

Isaiah 61:3

"To grant those who mourn in Zion, giving them a garland instead of ashes, the oil of gladness instead of mourning, the mantle of praise instead of a spirit of fainting."

Spring started to blossom, showing her long-awaited vibrant colors sprouting. The tree buds burst forth through the branches, and green grass sprouted from the ground. When I returned home, I couldn't wait to see my children and kiss Christian's chubby cheeks. To give a long-awaited embrace to my husband from a changed woman, wife, and mother who had transformed from the inside out. I wanted to hold him long and tight for the love he has shown me since the very beginning when we started dating.

Craig has been my rock through every season, every struggle, every triumph, and every tear. This has become our journey together. I couldn't imagine walking this journey with anyone else.

Lily and Landon greeted me, running outside and squealing with excitement as I pulled up to the curb. As I walked up to the front door, I could see my baby boy scooting around in his walker. In the waiting, my precious little one helped his mama step into extended healing. Christian's life had connected us to Samuel and Lucy in heaven in an incredible way to know them personally. These siblings here on earth and in heaven will always have a connection to one another no matter the distance between. I was HOME again, now a changed person through the grace, love, and mercy of my Heavenly Father.

There was a lot of excitement all at once as I walked through the door. As I embraced each of my children with kisses, I felt so blessed to have the family I have. I spotted the homemade "Welcome Home" sign spread on the dining room table, and Lily and Landon had made me homemade cards. Craig had bought me one of my favorite plants, an orchid. These little gifts were placed among a clean house with laundry done. The joy that I received at the retreat combined with even more joy from the love of my family was indescribable. I was overcome with all of God's goodness in everything. Even through the pain, His goodness still radiates.

Like pieces of a puzzle coming together to create a beautiful, unique masterpiece, so are the pieces that must slowly come together to reveal the fullness that is to take place in our own lives. The valleys of life are where we learn more about the character of the God we worship and serve. He will never be late or fail to keep His promises. His clock ticks to the rhythm of His heart and love. He is faithful!

About a month after the retreat, I pulled out the pastel flowered folder to skim through the papers and cards, reminiscing. I stopped at Samuel's birth certificate. I had forgotten the date I chose in January but was reminded on this day. I continued to look through the papers and read cards all addressed to "Lily." I felt the love that I was shown at the retreat all over again, overcome with how amazing that experience was for me.

I have tattoos of my children on my arm, and I had been wanting to add Samuel's as well. There was a scripture in the book of Samuel that seemed perfect, but I forgot exactly where it was so I looked it up. When I did, the numbers hit me, just as God has been speaking to me many times before with my birthday, the date of the abortion, and the time Samuel's picture was taken. God had been communicating through dates and times in the sweet symphony story.

For this child I prayed.
1 SAMUEL 1:27

I pulled out his birth certificate to see the date I had chosen. As much as God has shown Himself in so many details of my story, I shouldn't have been shocked by what I saw. However, a touch by God is not a feeling that gets old, nor is it something you get used to. Each touch is new, fresh, and unique. A touch from God is a glimpse from heaven, revealing in that moment that He is present all the time. We can't see Him, but we can feel Him more than ever in these moments. The feeling is breathtaking and extravagant. At times our flesh can turn into doubt, feeling that God is distant from us when life throws us curve balls. That's when God shows up, reminding us He is working all things out for good, encouraging us to hold on and not to lose hope.

Certificate of Life

Whereas on January 27, 2000, a baby boy was expected to be born of Ashlee Lynn Maloney Mincer, his natural mother and Craig Edward Mincer, his adoptive father.

As I saw numbers matching once again, tears of joy came forth. Samuel's birthday that I chose was January 27. The date I fumbled upon in frustration and longing was actually the date God was using not only for the Holy Spirit to fulfill the desires of my heart but also to fulfill His prophecy through my son.

The reference for this scripture in Samuel were the exact numbers for his birthday, 1/27. That morning that I decided on a date, I had no idea God was continuing to work. He knows our every thought. He knows our every desire.

Psalm 139:2

"You know when I sit and when I rise; You understand my thoughts from afar."

Psalm 37:4

"Delight yourself in the Lord; and He will give you the desires of your heart."

The only One who knew Samuel's birthday was God, Samuel's Creator who knit him in my womb. The only One who could reveal Samuel's birthday would be God. The Father saw me, knowing my thoughts and deepest desires when it came to my child I missed. Not only was this sign for me, but this sign also displays that Samuel's life has a purpose regarding the issue of abortion in our world.

Truth is, he has a birthday. He always had and always will in

God's book, even though it was erased here on earth. He never had the chance to shine his light here on earth. Instead, he is shining his light from above in another dimension, pouring heaven to earth to display the works and glory of God. God is declaring that every baby has a face, a name, and a birthday and is created uniquely, gifted to shine their light in this world.

Chapter 12 - Full Circle

In the month of May, while I was sitting outside enjoying the warmer weather about a month after the retreat, a dear friend of mine (sister in Christ) walked past. I had met Jennifer about three years prior in a Bible study at a friend's house. There were seasons we hadn't seen one another, yet we always had an instant connection, the kind of friendship that lasts no matter how much time passes. It's always so natural to pick up where we left off.

Smiles formed as our eyes met, excited to catch up on things in our lives. She had been healing after a major surgery while I had wanted to share my experience from the retreat. I couldn't wait to share the new, transformed Ashlee.

As Christian bounced on her lap, I began to tell her how much healing had transpired in many different areas and how I felt like a totally new person, completely free. I had traded mourning for joy, finally able to lay it all at Jesus's feet. I had been forgiven and set free!

After much excitement, her body language started to change.

Then, all of a sudden, as I could see the wheels turning inside her head, she began an unexpected conversation. She had known my story for a short period of time, maybe three to four months. When I shared it with her, I had no idea she worked for the local pregnancy center in our town. We had no idea what was working within our friendship for the future. We were connected for a divine appointment, soon to find out how God was connecting the dots.

All throughout my story, there were specific people strategically placed in my path for a purpose to guide and lead me to where the Author of my life saw me in the future. Our *presence* in the people around us is what makes a true impact, making a difference especially for those who are broken and crushed in spirit.

Presence is where we can be the hands and feet of Jesus. We are the compassion and body of Jesus here on earth, not only by helping someone who is going through a difficult time but to propel them into the place where God is leading them.

1 Corinthians 12:27

"Now you are Christ's body, and individually members of it."

"Ashlee, I don't know how to ask you this, so I am just going to come right out and ask," Jennifer stated, getting right to the point.

I became so curious, anticipating what she could possibly be going to ask me.

"We have a fundraiser for the pregnancy center coming up in October called 'Feel the Beat,' and we are looking for a keynote speaker. I know many who have had an abortion, but I keep coming back to you and your story, God's great story of redemption through you," Jennifer said.

This was the moment that God's prophetic promise of speaking would be fulfilled. Without an ounce of hesitation or fear, before she could even finish speaking, I silently said yes in my head. As soon as she finished, I said, with a smile filled with complete peace, "Yes, I would love to." I knew without a doubt this was from the Lord and that is what gave me fearless, joyous strength to say yes.

I am sure she was nervous asking me out of the blue if I would be able to step out into vulnerability and share my story so publicly. I reassured her I was confident in doing so because I knew without a doubt this was from God. It was the moment I was waiting for, His timing.

> Presence is where we can be the hands and feet of Jesus.

Only His hand could reach down and guide me back to my hometown to speak publicly, sharing my testimony for the very first time. The stretching I had experienced through the healing process strengthened me to get me to this place. I had been in purposeful preparation for nearly four years.

God didn't see my dark depravity as I lay there at the abortion clinic. He didn't see the young girl who felt completely worthless and too far gone in the crushed and mangled car resting in front of the tree. He saw me totally different from what the natural eye could see.

Through His eyes stood the woman I would grow into and become. My mistakes in life didn't define me, because they weren't my true identity. God saw my worth. My identity resided in His Son Jesus Christ who poured out His love and mercy over me through His shed blood.

I had about five months to write and prepare for my speech. As

I wrote my testimony, there was still healing through writing it. There has still been healing as I write this book as well. The difference between the healing before and now is God has strengthened me to be bold, courageous, and full of confidence, knowing my true identity. He has turned my pain into a passionate purpose. Unless we step into vulnerability, we will never be able to step into boldness and courageousness for God.

Joel 2:25

"Then I will make up to you for the years that the swarming locust has eaten, the creeping locust, the stripping locust and the gnawing locust, My great army which I sent among you."

After the abortion in my days of drinking and doing drugs, I got caught for underage drinking and was taken into the police station to do a breathalyzer test. I left that night sentenced to serving a certain number of hours in community service. Out of all places I could have picked to do those hours, I chose the pregnancy center.

Elaine was the director at the time. I was obviously seeking something, choosing to be there. Maybe I was curious to see what this pregnancy center offered. Maybe I was searching for someone to talk to. I shared my experience with Elaine. Being there probably helped me feel close to my baby in a small way.

She gave me a tour around the center while talking to me about what services they offered. It was in a small, light green house at the time, across from the local coffee shop. That house still sits there today with memories that I made there. This place felt inviting with a sense of home to it.

I remember the first day I was there, a young girl came in to take a pregnancy test. Quietly in my thoughts, I was longing for that option. *That could have been me.*

The hard reality that hit me as I saw that young girl was that it was too late for me. It was never meant to be for me.

The next thing I remember from my time at the center was helping sort through the baby clothes and items, putting the tiny clothes on baby hangers and hanging them on display in the baby boutique in the basement. What ifs and what could have been invaded my mind and the aching hole in my heart. But life must go on...

It's amazing how many details in our lives God can turn around. I was a little nervous heading to the pregnancy center to meet with the ladies there before my speech, yet at the same time in awe that God was bringing me full circle again.

I got out of my car and grabbed the diaper bag, swinging Christian on my hip to walk up to the center at its new location. It felt surreal. I was brought back to the place I could have gone to receive help more than eighteen years ago. Now, in God's timing, I was returning to share my testimony to help others.

Soon after I walked through the door, there was the baby boutique. Jennifer greeted me with a big hug, introducing me to everyone: Lynne, the director, Gracie, the bookkeeper, and Evie, client services director. They were so excited to meet me and hear my testimony that I would be sharing for the fundraiser. I still felt nervous and vulnerable to share everything about my past, but they were so inviting, attentive, wanting to make me feel comfortable sharing a very vulnerable and raw part of my life. Their sensitive compassion helped me to open up freely, holding nothing back. They had never met me before but displayed they truly cared for me. These women instantly felt like family to me.

Christian sat on my lap most of the time, eating his favorite cereal puffs and being so good the whole time. Time stood still, like I was there talking with them for minutes, not at least an hour and a half. Lynne, Jennifer, Evie, and Gracie's hearts poured over me like a fresh cleansing rain. They loved hearing my story while loving on me, knowing it would help so many. Before I left, they covered me in prayer. This would not be the only time they would pray over me. Their prayers to heaven helped me through the process up until the night of the fundraiser.

As Christian and I left, I was drawn to a picture of Elaine hanging by the front door. I had missed it when I walked in. I remembered her familiar face, wishing I would have been able to meet her again. She had passed away about a year prior. On the plaque with her picture it read, "Well done, my good and faithful servant." Elaine's legacy inspired me to keep fighting the good fight, serving God well.

Even though I didn't know her well, and she might not have remembered me, I knew she was looking down on me in that moment. I felt close to her like I had during the days I did my community service helping her. I know she has met Samuel in heaven, along with all of the children she hadn't been able to meet here on earth and help through her ministry.

I left that day with complete peace in God's plan to prepare me to share confidently, no matter how hard it was going to be for me. God had been building my maturity personally and spiritually. The pulling and stretching to the point of wanting to give up many times had brought me to this point. I knew without a doubt He would give me strength for that night, remembering again that when we are weak, He is made strong.

So many times through the journey, two words would arise: "Only God." Only God could have taken me on a four-year healing journey, paving the path for me to share my story publicly for the first time in my hometown. Only God could display mighty signs, wonders, and miracles in my life like He had. I never could have imagined or dreamed my life would turn from a dark, destructive, broken past to what it has—the most beautiful, amazing story of my life. His story.

For about five months, I plugged away, typing my testimony in between taking care of my kids on busy days filled with running Lily to tennis lessons and Landon to summer camp three days a week. Tickets for the fundraiser did not sell easily, to the point that they might not even breakeven for the cost of it. As it was getting closer with time running out, there was worry if everything would work out. The ladies decided to have a meeting. They made the confident decision that no matter what happened, they would not cancel this event. They wholeheartedly believed in me and in God's plan. It didn't matter if they sold five tickets or a hundred. They were not going to say no to God, knowing this night was all set up by my Heavenly Father. They knew I had been working so hard to prepare. They refused to give up when natural circumstances didn't look promising, refusing to let the enemy win. We know who holds our promises until they are fulfilled. In the end, God showed His faithfulness. As it got closer to the deadline to purchase tickets, sales started to quickly pick up.

The day of the fundraiser, I stepped into the Elk's Lodge as the banquet hall was being set up. The sign outside the building had greeted me with, "Welcome to 'Feel the Beat.'" The hard months of preparation became incredibly real in this moment. This was really happening. Everything that had transpired along the hard road had guided me to this day.

> So many times through the journey, two words would arise: "Only God."

I walked in to a sight I wasn't expecting. Sudden surprise hit like the day of the memorial service at the retreat. Tears suddenly came as I was overcome with so much emotion at the beautiful display being prepared for that evening. Tears dripped down my face in thankfulness, praise, joy, and huge relief that I made it this far without quitting when times were really hard.

White linen and black and red satin draped the elegantly-decorated tables and chairs, as if decked out for a wedding reception. The detail put into this evening was just like the memorial service that God had planned for me, breathtaking in its elegance and beauty.

Craig met me there to help after working some hours at his second job delivering pizzas. Being the technical guy he is, he made sure the PowerPoint and laptop were set up correctly. The nerves were hitting me. I never liked having eyes on me, let alone having to talk in front of an audience about abortion.

In just a few hours, I was going to be completely outside of my comfort zone again. The words that were still hard to say would inevitably have to come out this evening that, "I had an abortion."

After a quick run-through, we needed to head out to get ready. I didn't have much time to feel the nerves now. As I got myself ready, Craig watched Christian and went over directions with the babysitter. We put our formal clothes in Lily's room to change into right before we snuck out the back door so Christian wouldn't get upset seeing us leave. We seized the moment when Christian was distracted, changed our wardrobe quietly, and slipped out the back door. We stopped to take a quick selfie in the back yard before heading to the hall. This was it. There was no turning back.

After a delicious dinner, Lynne opened the speaking portion of the evening and introduced me. Standing at the podium while the PowerPoint was loading, I felt peace. I felt God's strength pulling me through to do what He had been calling me to. This was ultimately His night, His orchestration. It was time to shine God's light and glory. I had rehearsed over and over so I felt ready, but as I started and eyes were on me, the nerves came. A few sentences in, Jennifer pointed to her ear, indicating they couldn't hear me well. I tried to adjust the mic but was too short for it to reach closer to my mouth. This wasn't going to work.

I talked silently in my head, *Okay, Ashlee. It's time to adjust. You just need to hold the mic. You have no other option.* It threw me off a bit yet I was able to get back on my feet. Then came the most difficult words to speak. I was struggling to keep it together and get the words out as I fought back tears.

With a deep breath in and exhale out, intense surrender came. "This is my abortion story and my journey to healing."

I glanced at my hand to see what I wrote as a reminder from God. His strength would get me through this.

Esther 4:14

"For such a time as this."

As I ended with my final words, a huge weight of relief fell off. Tears broke out as I put the mic down on the podium. As Lynne wrapped her arms around my neck, she said "I am so proud of you. God loves you, and I love you."

I felt comforted after feeling complete vulnerability, exposing hidden and dark experiences in my life. The audience gave a round of applause to show their support for me. As I held onto Lynne, I thought to myself, *I did it, God. I did it. You got me through like You told me You would.*

I was overwhelmed both by the women and men who came up to me and the words they expressed. Some were in tears, crying on my shoulder and whispering how my story had touched them so much and how they had been affected in some way with abortion. This is why we take up our cross, bearing the uncomfortableness, to reach people. The vulnerability is worth it to help people on their journey when they need help, hope, and healing. Being obedient to the call will produce God's bright light shining through us to be a voice providing an extraordinary solution to someone else's need.

We are called to:

- *proclaim good news*
- *proclaim freedom for people who are imprisoned*
- *help people who are imprisoned by the enemy's lies*
- *help people who are spiritually and physically blind*
- *set the oppressed free*

On my journey, God had placed a burning desire on my heart to see from His perspective. He has taught me to continually look up, come up, and rise up, looking from heaven's perspective in order to see things clearly. It's only by doing things at high altitudes that we get used to the height needed to soar.

Isaiah 40:31

"Yet those who wait for the Lord will gain new strength; they will mount up with wings like eagles, they will run and not get tired, they will walk and not become weary."

There is no reason to fear the height. We need never fall for the lie that God isn't currently fully engaged and active in our lives, even when we can't see what He is doing behind the clouds.

Chapter 13 - Hannah: For This Child I Prayed

Accepting my past and the way I lost my son was very difficult. For many seasons, I didn't want to accept it because I longed for my child so much. It was too hard to bear. I did not want to accept that it was all in God's plan.

My heart was filled with overwhelming joy and thankfulness for the miracle God had given me, yet my heart still anguished in deep despair for everything that I lost, especially my son's presence and to know him. The truth is that if we can't accept our past, we will never be truly able to move forward in all of the fullness God has for us.

Psalm 139:16

"Your eyes have seen my unformed substance; and in Your book were all written the days that were ordained for me, when as yet there was not one of them."

This scripture is undeniably powerful when we look at our lives. In many ways, this truth can be hard to face. Samuel was taken far too early, yet God knew the abortion was coming. Before He formed Samuel in my womb, He knew him. He could see ahead to the sin that was going to occur at the abortion clinic. Yet God was working, mastering His plan for Samuel and me.

Even though I now knew God's plan was to use my son's sacrifice as a banner of His Glory to shine on the darkness of abortion, it still took me quite some time to fully accept and be able to heal. The retreat was the final resting place for all of my guilt, shame, sorrow, and regret. It was the place I came to true acceptance of God's plan through the suffering in my life.

God brought Samuel's precious and innocent face to earth not only in response to a mother's deep yearning and heart cry for her child but for the world to see. His picture became a beacon of truth and life, shown on behalf of the millions of lives aborted—lives God created in His image uniquely, perfectly, and purposefully.

God pours heaven to earth to show Himself and His heart. His heart breaks over the deceptive blindness of abortion in our world and culture. Father God does not create a tool unless He has a specific plan and purpose for it. We are all planned and planted for heavenly purposes within the kingdom of God. Sometimes He can plant His seeds in the worst soil because in our weakness, He is made strong. In our weakness, we receive God's strength and grace to push through and carry on. Miracles are made in and through our weaknesses and brokenness. There can be purpose planted in loss, grief, and suffering.

I can relate to Hannah's despair and heart cry up to heaven with a deep longing for a child. My prayer consisted of the same longing and anguish to know my child. Inevitably, there will be times we will have to let go of the ones we love far too soon— for many, sooner than expected. My silence for fifteen years didn't discount my love for my child or discount his dignity and worth. It was always there.

Only God knew the inner aches of my soul, just like Hannah's with every beat of our hearts. Hannah and I shared a similar feeling of barrenness and emptiness. While I lost my child, the Lord closed Hannah's womb to be a chosen vessel to give birth to a prophet but at the right time.

Isaiah 66:9

"'Shall I bring to the point of birth and not give delivery?' says the Lord. 'Or shall I who gives delivery shut the womb?' says your God."

God reverses barrenness on the basis of His nature, preparing Hannah and me for the precise time to fulfill His promises. God reversed my barrenness from abortion with a miracle in response to my heartsick cry, not physically like Hannah but by His supernatural power from heaven.

> God pours heaven to earth to show Himself and His heart.

1 Samuel 1:21-22

"Then the man Elkanah went up with all his household to offer to the Lord the yearly sacrifice and pay his vow. But Hannah did not go up, for she said to her husband, 'I will not go up until the child is weaned; then I will bring him, that he may appear before the Lord and stay there forever.'"

In the same way Hannah dedicated her son Samuel to God, so has been the outcome of my story. I just didn't know it was coming. God knew my Samuel was going to be taken so shortly after he was conceived, sending him straight back to heaven in the arms of Jesus. My son was separated, called, and chosen before he was conceived. My suffering was already written in place to endure before my son even came to be. Hannah's suffering was written before her Samuel ever came to be.

The reality of God's truth in my life and Samuel's life in the Bible took time to understand and comprehend. The truth that the loss of my son was in God's plan took intense, deep, cutting acceptance and healing. I endured searing agony through the process of total surrender, letting go of my son and what could have been. What could have been was never meant to be and that took tremendous heart-wrenching acceptance on my part as his mother. But this life-changing sorrow built my complete trust in God, allowing me to accept the truth and understand that there was always a greater purpose for my pain.

Hannah's son was a prophet who exhorted Israel to turn from idolatry and serve God alone. In Samuel's time, people were destroyed by their own selfishness. Since the landmark decision in 1973, when the United States Supreme Court ruled in favor of abortion through Roe vs. Wade, we have been destroying innocent lives of children every day. I have been shown through the years on this journey that my son is a prophet to the nations for the world to turn from the lies of abortion to God's truth. Just as Samuel directed people back to God, so He is using my son to redirect our nation back to Him, turning from the legalization and abomination of abortion.

God will pour out heaven on earth to shake what must be shaken. We can avoid the corruption of this world if we place God first. Samuel's life serves as an example for believers today that justice is administered through obedience to God, faith, and willingness to intercede for others. My son was predestined to intercede for the unborn. I haven't met my son yet, but this mama is so, so proud of him and the person he was created to be, despite the tremendous pain of the piece missing from my life.

Jeremiah 1:5

"Before I formed you in the womb I knew you, and before you were born I consecrated you; I have appointed you a prophet to the nations."

In the picture, my son was even dressed to represent the prophet Samuel in the Bible. He is wearing a dark black coat over his vibrant orange shirt, another detail I didn't quite understand for a long time. In the same way that God revealed the meaning behind the color of his shirt, He eventually revealed through scripture why my son was dressed in the attire he was.

1 Samuel 2:19

"And his mother would make him a little robe and bring it to him from year to year when she would come up with her husband to offer the yearly sacrifice."

I stand in continued awe of God's ways and nature. These purposeful details were discovered slowly through the hills and valleys on the journey, through intimacy and communion with the Holy Spirit.

> God will pour heaven on earth to shake what must be shaken.

Through this journey, I have had to face the gripping reality that no matter how badly I wanted to keep my child, he was already set apart and separated from me. Samuel transcends light in the darkness of abortion carrying God's glory to change hearts. His picture of heaven touching earth illuminates the sanctity of life of the unborn and millions of babies that have been aborted. They are alive and well in the kingdom of heaven on streets of gold.

Nothing could have prepared me for the miracle blessing He had for me. That is why it is called a *MIRACLE*. I didn't request anything in prayer. His immense mercy touched me out of my darkest despair. God can use human weakness to accomplish great things.

In the story of Hannah, we can see that God knows our story from beginning to end, that everything has a purpose. Putting our trust in Him is never unaccounted for. God is already in the future as He patiently waits for us to catch up.

Chapter 14 - Chosen

Before we ever came to be, each one of us had a roadmap in advance for our destiny and the good works we would do to fulfill it. A story as already written over our lives before we existed. Blueprints of our destiny were already etched in the stone road. He will give us strength for the journey with a new sense of direction to the assignment set in place. We must be willing to learn perseverance, humility, and courage. Through the storms of life, God works in the depths of our character to sustain what we are called to step into. We won't be perfect. We will stumble, and we will break at times. But let's not forget His grace is sufficient and faithful. God wants us to unlock the doors to go from glory to glory to the place He has already seen us arrive.

1 Peter 2:9

"But you are a chosen race a royal priesthood, a holy nation, a people for God's own possession, so that you may proclaim the excellencies of Him who has called you out of darkness into His marvelous light."

I will admit I often questioned, "Why me?" Especially in the beginning when I got the picture of Samuel. I am just your average girl from a small town in Ohio. I never imagined how good my life would become when I made that decision to follow Jesus. I truly knew better than to question my Heavenly Father, Creator of the wide spans of heaven and earth. There were times I couldn't help but think that of all the people on this planet who could have been used, He chose me, a mere speck on this enormous earth. Literally, a needle in a haystack. God doesn't see us in that way. I needed not only to be taught through scripture truth in my life but also to *believe* that I was chosen for this unique assignment. To *believe* my story was all in His design, even if I didn't sign up for it.

Looking back on my past, specifically at the point of my accident, I was blinded to God's nature. I didn't know His character, love, mercy, and grace for me, or that He could override the mistakes and sin in my life to replace them with a sweet symphony of love and a complete turnaround. Nevertheless, I was always being sought after, never alone nor forsaken in the biggest battle of my life. The battle I was fighting on the ground was never mine to fight, a war I could never possibly win on my own. The weight was too much for me to bear to go on another moment. The battle had already been won on the cross of Calvary. For me to win took my complete surrender, intentionally saying YES over and over again.

We are chosen for a designated path on earth to do mighty exploits to display God working in our lives and point others to their salvation. What is predestined is what we will become after we are saved. Salvation is a one-time experience, yet the walk is continual. He doesn't want us to stop at salvation alone. We were designed to grow sustaining, deep roots in our faith, trusting and believing we were built for Him to use in ways that only He can. We will discover purpose in our lives when we listen, obey, and trust Him.

Ashlee who was lost, alone, and damaged to the point of death was not the same Ashlee who would blossom and emerge through the years as she followed her Heavenly Daddy. God's steadfast patience enabled me to blossom into a beautiful, orange lily on fire for God, soaring into the woman He created me to be. Through the journey, I didn't always believe in myself, but God always believed in me.

Nothing can hinder what God has prepared for us. When we can see our life the way God sees, from heaven's perspective, we will know with confidence that His plans for our lives will come to pass.

The mission will cost us something. Taking a risk won't feel good. It will entail deciding to take up our cross, no matter the cost. It's important to stay grounded as we move through the seasons of chaos, growth, and transition. What joy it will bring when we embrace the purpose we were created for, to reach those who need to be reached, to make an impact for the kingdom. It will burden our hearts if we don't follow it. We have to want to fulfill it. He will not force it on us.

"Why me?" should never be a question in our identity in Christ. "Why not me?" is what we should be saying boldly and confidently. It's something I had to live and learn.

Each of our callings are unique and one of a kind. Joseph's preparation was one of a kind. He would have never ruled and reigned if he lived in doubt, especially in his darkest days in prison. Our pain has meaning by bringing glory to God. Our pain can be connected to someone else's healing and salvation. If God can use me, He can use anyone. He can turn anyone's situation around, no matter how far gone you might be. We will need to rely on the Holy Spirit to guide and interpret the vision clearly in order to receive and declare it.

Ezekiel 22:30

*"I searched for a man among them who would build up the wall and stand
in the gap."*

Many times, the Father uses broken vessels to reach our broken
world. He often selects weak and unlikely people who are simply
willing for God. When we hide or run from our past, we are
postponing someone else's breakthrough and their freedom
through Jesus Christ. Let's take a look at some of the unlikely
people God used to accomplish His will, advance the gospel,
and ultimately reveal His glory.

Noah

Noah and his family appeared to be the only righteous people
on earth after the fall of man in the Garden of Eden. After the
fall, the world became increasingly evil.
God told Noah to build an arc that he,
his family, and two of every bird and
land animal would live in to survive the
coming flood and repopulate the world.

> Nothing can
> hinder what
> God has
> prepared
> for us.

After the flood, Noah planted a vineyard
and not only became drunk but also naked. Even though God
knew Noah was going to act sinfully, He still used him in a
mighty way to build an arc nearly one and a half football fields
long to withstand the flood and repopulate. Not only did God
know of his future sin, but He was patient in the years Noah
took to complete his assignment.

Moses

Moses was chosen by God to bring his people back from
captivity in Egypt. A stutterer was chosen to speak. Moses even
told God he was not good with words and never had been. He
got tongue-tied easily, words getting tangled, yet God used him
anyway, reminding Moses He would always be by his side.

Saul

Another unlikely person was Saul, who later became known as the Apostle Paul. Saul, who was originally a Pharisee and a very well-known religious leader among the Jewish community, would often harm or kill anyone who claimed to be Christian. It wasn't until he had a vision from Jesus that he turned his life around to follow and serve Christ. Paul's story of redemption and total transformation is proof God can use anyone, despite their past.

1 Corinthians 1:26-29

"For consider your calling, brethren, that there were not many wise according to the flesh, not many mighty, not many noble; but God has chosen the foolish things of the world to shame the wise, and God has chosen the weak things of the world to shame the things which are strong, and the base things of the world and the despised God has chosen, the things that are not, so that He may nullify the things that are, so that no man may boast before God."

I stand in awe and wonder seeing how God has chosen my husband and all of my children in their own special intentional way in my journey. Each member of my family has been a true gift through the healing. I wouldn't be where I am today if it weren't for them.

Craig was the man God had saved for me to marry and have a beautiful family with. I can't express enough how much Craig's heart has embraced me, my son in heaven, and the hills and valleys leading to healing and wholeness. His strength and unconditional love to endure this process with me is not for everyone. Never once did he waiver when the next set of tears came from more areas of trauma that needed to be tended to. His selfless heart has loved so deeply to call my son his own, with a love that comes from the heart of God.

It's amazing to see how God has been working in and through my children's lives, showing His presence strongly in Lily's life. I can say I was chosen to be Lily's mama, but really Lily was chosen for me just as much. She was set apart even before she was formed in my belly. Just like my husband, Lily was also entrusted with an important role in God's story. He gifted her even when she was too young to be aware or understand the magnitude of it. Lily was 7 years old when the Holy Spirit led her to discover God's miracle picture to show me at the precise time.

At the time, she was too young to tell about all the details of the story. I kept it simple, that mommy lost a baby in my tummy and that was her big brother in heaven. I explained that I was sad and prayed to God about the baby I lost. God gave me a very special miracle with a picture of him in the same exact place mommy said her prayer. Her brother was happy in heaven with Jesus. Lily understood and was really amazed at what God had done. *She believed.* We discussed that this experience was special to our family and to be kept within our family.

Through the next four years, Lily would ask about her older brother every now and then while getting out the Nintendo DS to look at his picture. It wasn't until a few months before the speech that I shared everything with her as Craig and I felt she was old enough to hear more.

Landon was at his day summer camp at the time. Lily and I were taking Christian for a walk when I brought up that there was more to Samuel's story. There was a greater purpose for why God wanted me to share my testimony to others. I told her if she would like to know, we could talk about it when we got home while Christian took a nap. She said she would like that.

As we sat on the couch close to one another, I told her how Samuel passed away in my belly, explaining to her what abortion was. Sadness filled her after hearing the hard truth. At 11 years old, she understood everything I was telling her.

The moment came when I had to tell her that her daddy was not Samuel's daddy. I could tell it didn't quite click when I said I was 18 when I lost him. It hadn't registered in her mind that Samuel didn't look like her daddy. In her innocence, Craig is the only daddy she knows. When I delved deeper, more tears started to fill her eyes and she wrapped her arms around me. As her head nestled into my chest, the tears started streaming. In that moment, I thought maybe I made a mistake telling her too soon. My daughter's heart was hurting so much right now. She reassured me it was okay.

In that specific moment, something hit her tender heart. All the pieces of the story came together all at once. In that tight embrace, she displayed that her heart missed her older brother in heaven more than ever. It didn't matter to her that he was her half-brother. To her, he was her older brother no matter the circumstances. That's childlike faith right there.

After our embrace, while shedding tears together, she quickly got up, running to her room. Surprised, I wondered what the urgency was all about. She took a picture of the two of us out of a small purple frame, wanting to put Samuel's picture in it instead. From that day on, she held his picture close to her. She still sleeps with it every night. The purple frame is even packed with her when she's away from home. Samuel is never far from her to see and hold.

We continued our heart-to-heart and the sad reality that abortion is legal in America. I expressed what God wants for us and how He wants to use us to make an impact not only in people's lives but in the world. She had a better understanding now why mommy had been preparing for months, typing and practicing my speech. She could see now that our brokenness can help others in their own healing and journey with God.

There would be times, especially at night right before bed, when deep sorrow would consume Lily. Deep sadness would creep in because Samuel wasn't here with us. It was evident she yearned for the presence of her brother to hold her and talk to her when she was upset with situations at school or with friends. She wanted to have the presence of her big brother watch over her, to help her through life's struggles. A brother, protector, and forever friend she could count on was taken from her, and she felt the loss deeply. God spoke to me one night as a huge crocodile tear slipped down her nose onto her pillow and she held onto his picture tightly.

The Lord whispered wisdom,

"Ashlee, I knew Lily's pure heart before I formed her in your womb. I set her apart for this role in my story before she ever came to be. Only I could see in the future that she wouldn't take this miracle for granted. I saw in advance how her heart would ache for the piece that is missing, the piece I created that was not a mistake. She would see truth in her brother's story. I ENTRUSTED this miracle to her."

That was a powerful moment when that grieving tear dripped of those words.

Journal Entry 2/4/19

Dear God,

Help Craig and me to continue to lead our children to You. I pray for leading and protection for all of them. I pray Lily starts to feel joy more instead of mourning, but I know she is grieving as well and in her time. What a gift she is. Help me to rest in You, God.

In Jesus's Name, Amen

The result of abortion is a domino effect for generations. We don't realize how many it will impact for years, even decades, down the road. For so long I lived in a reality that my aborted child would never be spoken of, never be remembered. I certainly never had plans for my children to know I had an abortion or that they had a half sibling in heaven. It was never a thought in my mind. My plan was to keep this silenced forever. But that was never in God's plan.

One Sunday, Lily talked about what she learned in church. She said they learned it in the book of Samuel.

She said, matter of fact, "Samuel in the Bible taught people about God, and our Samuel is teaching people about God."

And just as simple and true as that, she gets it. Out of the mouths of babes shines *childlike faith*. Lily has displayed this faith throughout God's story. So, what is childlike faith? Let's look in Matthew to delve deeper.

Matthew 18:1-6

"At that time the disciples came to Jesus and said, 'Who then is greatest in the kingdom of heaven?' And He called a child to Himself and set him before them, and said, 'Truly I say to you, unless you are converted and become like children, you will not enter the kingdom of heaven. Whoever then humbles himself as this child, he is the greatest in the kingdom of heaven. And whoever receives one such child in My name receives Me; but whoever causes one of these little ones who believe in Me to stumble, it would be better for him to have a heavy millstone hung around his neck, and to be drowned in the depth of the sea.'"

Childlike and *childish* have two vastly different meanings. Yet, as we grow and develop, we display both. To be *childish*, we display immaturity, obnoxiousness, selfishness, and at times lack of emotional restraint. This doesn't just pertain to children. We've all been at a place of losing our cool when we should push back our feelings and look to God for how we should react.

Childlike has many positive, beautiful words to describe it. Children trust and forgive more easily than adults can. Children have wonder, curiosity, innocence, and carefree joy. Children are eager to know everything, eager to know the truth in things. Adults, on the other hand, can sometimes ask so many questions, have an ulterior motive, want to challenge and get into a debate. These things then lead to being confrontational and passive aggressive.

Children do not fear their reputation or image nor who is around them. Childlike faith asks honest questions with no hidden agenda. Faith like a child asks openly with vulnerability. A child doesn't always know what is best for them but trusts their parents with satisfaction. Children have an incredible capacity to trust, sometimes leading them into harmful situations unless they are taught otherwise. It doesn't matter if the child is hurt or frustrated. They know to trust their parents as they show them love through it.

> The result of abortion is a domino effect for generations.

Do we have that childlike faith, truly living it out in our lives? At times we stumble, knowing we need to redirect ourselves to the Father because, ultimately, we know He knows what is best for us, even when we cannot see. When life gets really hard or answers are not right in front of us, can we truly let everything go? Letting go of our plans, of how we think God will turn things around, and of wanting control when the turbulence comes can be hard. Yet, it's possible.

What the enemy means to break us, God means to build us through Jesus Christ. We are stronger than we realize as Christ resides in us. Our spirit is alive because of His righteousness. When we are weak, He is strong, holding us up with His righteous right hand. When we fall, feeling defeated, that's when our childlike faith comes in, trusting God has it already taken care of.

The awesome, mind-blowing nature of God is that He will totally flip our ideas and plans upside-down. He will do anything to reach us, heal us, and deliver us. He will do anything in His power to show Himself not only in our own lives but our children's lives as well as others around us. God exposes the dark, hidden secrets and sin to break our bondage, revealing His truth and glory.

Ephesians 5:13-14

"But all things become visible when they are exposed by the light, for everything that becomes visible is light. For this reason it says, 'Awake, sleeper, and arise from the dead, and Christ will shine on you.'"

Babies that are aborted are often forgotten, never to be remembered. The faceless and nameless ones that are tragically discarded in a horrific way are important and loved by God. Heaven wants to shine the light of these children who very much have faces, have names, and are alive and well in the kingdom of heaven. To expose the corrupt and deceptive truth of abortion will allow healing for generations to come.

Not only did He want me to heal and be whole but also to bring forth what was hidden from my daughter and sons so they could see the glory of God, the truth about abortion, and know they have a big brother in heaven with their sister. They wouldn't have to endure that missing piece in their lives until they would meet in heaven. God doesn't want us to live with any pieces missing. Heaven can come to earth. Yes, it's more than possible with God—on earth as it is in heaven.

Despite circumstances seen or unseen, there is value in all life. For Samuel, there were both seen and unseen circumstances.

The seen, or known, were the words spoken from the rheumatologist that I couldn't get pregnant on this medication because the baby would have serious birth defects. Rightfully so, these words are enough to scare anyone into fear and panic mode. The unseen in Samuel's story was him—totally hidden, tucked away safe, growing inside my womb. God's plan for Samuel's life was unseen. An ultrasound was never done to show if there really was something wrong or if he was perfectly healthy. That was the deceptive aspect of the abortion clinic. They claim to have been helping me with my situation to "solve the problem," yet they never educated me on anything in regard to my situation. Particularly, they didn't even care to check the health and development of my child.

Regardless of what the outcome might have been, there was no proof. Even if something was wrong, that does not justify ending his life. God proves a very valid point through Samuel's story: every life has worth and the right to life. The clinic never had the right to decide my child's fate, whether there was an ultrasound or not. They knew my circumstance yet selfishly chose not to share any information with me about my pregnancy or any other possible options. That is not women's reproductive rights at all. If I was old enough to have an abortion on my own, I should have had the right to visibly see my son on an ultrasound to make that decision for myself. I was never given that option.

> Despite circumstances seen or unseen, there is value in all life.

God has a purpose for every life. If Craig and I knew our son Landon would be born perfectly healthy only to regress into autism, would we have aborted him? Would we have made that decision because of the foreseen circumstances fifteen months down the road? Absolutely not! All life is worth living. Aborting Samuel, who may have had birth defects or been disabled, didn't mean I would never have a child who wasn't "typical" or would endure challenges in life. We were still faced with a child with special needs. Samuel's life and Landon's life both had unforeseen and hidden circumstances.

What caused the autism doesn't matter anymore. What matters is Landon's life has great value, worthy to be lived, and he has taught us so much on this journey called life. The many valuable lessons we have learned through the eyes of autism have made us better individuals and parents. Even though many years have been unbelievably hard for Lily, she has developed a sensitivity and love for the special needs community. She naturally gravitates toward these children with her tender heart of compassion.

Landon was also set apart and chosen in Gods' story in his own personal and unique way, just as Samuel, Craig, and Lily were. Landon's diagnosis may not have been a part of our plan, but God had unforeseen circumstances heading our way to work for good. Landon's regression put a long hold on our plans for a third child. The long wait was ultimately part of the grand orchestration leading to the perfect divine time for our family to be blessed with Christian. Years of a long pause were divine timing for more healing to be pulled to the surface. So many times, we wonder why God isn't doing anything to change our circumstances when, in fact, He is working harder than ever behind the scenes, lining things up for growth, strength, blessings, and purpose in the future.

Life is a gift in the most purist form, intentionally birthing meaning into the world. Life holds intentional heavenly purpose and plans for us to be connected to those around us. Sometimes we need to stop looking at the hardships in front of us and instead think outside of the box in the place where God makes big things happen.

When I look at Christian's beaming smile as he laughs, I see God's goodness in the years of waiting. There was goodness being worked in and through all the years of pain and trauma endured. I never imagined this child would be a part of our family. I certainly never imagined he would be a huge part of bringing more healing to the surface at just the right season. He is truly a beautiful gift from God.

Memories that I could have had with Samuel in this house triggered my mind to daydreaming a lot. God has restored what the enemy took from me in an amazing way, turning my life full circle. Christian's vibrant life forced more hidden grief to surface that had become buried through the years when I thought I was okay. The season when I did the retreat Samuel, would have been 18, the exact age I was when I had to say goodbye to him before I even knew him.

At the same time, Christian's very being was starting to breathe new life into me again. My healing wouldn't have come without all the pieces slowly coming together. Each puzzle piece had an intricate part to play especially the lives that were chosen to be a part of God's story.

Chapter 15 –
Shine Your Light

When God calls you to something, it won't always be easy or feel very pleasant. I have certainly found this out through the years. It takes vulnerability to the point that we might question if we can actually do what He is asking of us. However, when God takes our brokenness and turns it into a beautiful story (Isaiah 61:3), we are called to break the barriers of our fear to share with others who need hope, healing, and deliverance. His glory was always meant to put on display to fill this broken world. This allows us to share the God who has transformed and restored us through our brokenness.

Will we leave the past behind and write the pages of history with the only One who can connect what needs to be connected? God our Creator is the only One who can make all of the chapters of our life come together. This happens when we allow Him into our hearts afresh to heal, restore, and fill us with the freedom that is only found in and through Jesus. The page of your life that you might feel is the ending will be a brand-new beginning with God. Turn the page to hope and allow your heart to be healed and dream again. It is when we endure the fiery fire that we will walk out pure as gold (1 Peter 1:7). We will become refined as a pure vessel able to boldly testify of the reason for the hope and faith within us.

When we confidently walk in heaven's calling, mandate, and

purpose, we will be given power and authority on earth to create change. We need to choose to rise out of the ashes of our past, come out of hiding to where transformation occurs, and live in agreement with God's promises over our lives. When we give ourselves and our lives into God's hands, He will make us a carrier of His glory. He is a behind-the-scenes kind of God. Just because things appear as a "no" or are delayed doesn't mean they are denied.

It's important to know that our Father wants us to come as we are. It's no surprise to Him that we aren't perfect and are a work in progress. However, that doesn't mean that He can't work in our lives and in ways we never could even imagine! We won't be perfect and blameless until we are in heaven, so keep pressing forward even with your imperfections or setbacks. God is for you. He will fight for you.

Every promise has a process to endure. When we stay planted and rooted in the vine, in time we will see victory over our circumstances. The enemy wants us down and bound forever. When we get up, rising from the inside, the enemy is defeated and victory will be won from the inside out. We can become the most determined and fearless fighters against the enemy to be able to free others still living under his insidious lies of manipulation and deception.

Seasons of growth perfect our faith. Giants are defeated as fear is defeated. Yes, at times faith can be a constant struggle, swaying us from here to there through the storms. But faith is also our solid foundation of hope and in our salvation.

Ephesians 2:8

"For by grace you have been saved through faith; and that not of yourselves, it is the gift of God."

The walk of faith is continual, growing and expanding deeper and deeper as we experience the power of God's presence and wisdom. There is hope from our dark, damaged, and regrettable pasts. When we trust like a child in God's promises, nothing will be wasted. He will use everything for good.

Our authority increases as we walk in obedience in our Lord. We have authority in and through Him. We have been given influence, power, and authority for a reason. We could be waiting tables, raising children, pursuing a full-time career, or leading an organization or ministry. Our "title" in life does not affect our ability to use our position of authority in Christ to make an impact on those we come in contact with.

Are we willing to step out and give back to Him for all that He has done for us? Can we say we will be His disciples, denying ourselves to take up our cross (Mark 8:34) and follow Him, knowing our reward in heaven will be to hear, "Well done, my good and faithful servant, well done"?

> Every promise has a process to endure.

One touch from God can change things within us that seasons of counseling cannot. I am not saying there is anything wrong or negative about counseling. There are many benefits to therapy, especially in regard to trauma, and I received it for many years on and off.

But through my experience, only One Person knew my deepest roots of pain that I wasn't even aware of, those hidden areas only He can see to pull out of us. He knows us that intimately to our core. Our ultimate and complete healing is through Jesus's blood shed freely for us. Life can get unbelievably messy and chaotic. God understands our healing on earth may not be instantaneous. That is why He leads us to other believers to provide resources that only He could arrange. He will bring others alongside us who have experienced and endured the journey that we are walking through.

God will sometimes allow us to get worn out to the point that we learn total dependence upon Him. He allows this so we understand the difference between our own strength and His strength that He gives us. I was worn out countless times in my story, yet that is truly where the surrender took place. It's the place where you fully look to God, surrendering to a plan you cannot see. In the worn-out stage, you can wholeheartedly feel His embrace around you, holding you up, carrying you until you see the light at the end of the tunnel.

The pressing and pressure is not the end. Life's tribulations are not intended to diminish our purpose. They arise as God prepares us to get to the next stepping-stone. The pressing and pressure will awaken a dormant inner strength that we didn't know we had.

2 Corinthians 4:8-9

We are afflicted in every way, but not crushed; perplexed, but not despairing; persecuted, but not forsaken; struck down, but not destroyed."

When you are important to God, you are important to the enemy. Thieves don't break into empty houses. The enemy wouldn't be attacking if something valuable wasn't inside of you. Prepare for the battle at hand, putting on the full armor to take a stand against the enemy's schemes. Exercising faith that no weapon formed against us shall prosper.

- *belt of truth*
- *breastplate of righteousness*
- *feet fitted with readiness that comes from the gospel of peace*
- *shield of faith*
- *helmet of Salvation*
- *sword of the spirit*

All of what I have shared in my story is what I had to live through and learn with God's leading. It has been quite *the journey* so far, and I know He is not finished yet. I can't wait to see what He has in store for the future. I may not know the future like my King in heaven, but what I do know is this:

Philippians 1:6

"For I am confident of this very thing, that He who began a good work in you will perfect it until the day of Christ Jesus."

Victory is ours through Christ Jesus.

He has made everything beautiful in His time.

We endure walking through the road to healing so we can in turn be an example of hope for others that it can be done. We must endure the burning process to be able to come out on the other side shining like gold, strong

> Life's tribulations are not to diminish our purpose.

and confident, equipped to be the hands and feet of Jesus to others who are broken and hurting. We need to set ourselves free to be able to help set someone else free. Fruit does not come forth without labor. Then, life will be lived with passion and purpose "for such a time as this."

Matthew 5:16

"Let your light shine before men in such a way that they may see your good works, and glorify your Father who is in heaven."

Reflection Questions:

1. Are you post-abortive? Do you experience triggers that leave you with guilt and grief, many times fighting back tears? For instance, birthdays, anniversaries, and funerals?

2. Do you feel hopeless to accept forgiveness for yourself after an abortion?

3. Do you feel you have taken the necessary steps to healing in order to arrive at the place of accepting true forgiveness, feeling redeemed and setting yourself free from your past?

Resources:

For confidential pregnancy education, support, resources and active guidance for unplanned pregnancies.

Heartbeat Hope Medical
1243 Napoleon St.
Fremont OH 43420
(419)334-9079
http://www.friendsofheartbeat.org/

Heartbeat of Ottawa County
1848 East Perry St., Suite 20 PO Box 903
Port Clinton OH 43452
(419)-734-9359
http://www.heartbeatpc.org/

PROLIFE Across AMERICA
Get the post-abortive support you need by calling

1-800-366-7773

If you have experienced depression and have had thoughts of harming yourself or suicide please reach out and receive help. You are not alone.

National Suicide Prevention Lifeline
1-800-273-8255

Acknowledgments

I would like to first thank my Heavenly Father. God, You are not only my Creator, Redeemer, and Savior, but You have become my greatest friend. Thank You for Your unending love and patience with me on this journey called life. Words cannot express my gratitude for what Your Son Jesus endured on the cross for me and my sin. I am forever grateful for the cross and Your story over my life. I continue to stand in awe of You and who You are.

Next, I would like to thank my husband, Craig, for his unending support to me since day one. Your love displayed by the way you embraced this healing journey with me is a true testament of God's great love and compassion. Never once did you waiver. Thank you for accepting me for me and all the flaws in between. I am so grateful to have a husband and best friend to encourage me to step out of my comfort zone into God's greater purpose.

I am forever grateful for the two pregnancy centers God led me to for further healing—Heartbeat Hope Medical of Fremont, Ohio, and Heartbeat of Ottawa County. I am thankful for all of the ladies involved in my journey at both facilities who displayed their loving care and compassion that helped me endure such a painful area in my life. Thank you for being the hands and feet of Jesus to help me walk through the pain of trauma and loss.

A huge thank you goes to my true Dream Defender, Renee

Fisher. I am so grateful for your heart and ministry helping me to be able to self-publish. Thank you for believing in me on this journey and our prayer time.

Lastly I would like to thank Nelly Murariu for her amazing talent designing my book cover. You brought to life my vision in a breathtaking way.

About the Author

Ashlee Mincer has been happily married to her husband Craig for fourteen years. She proudly wears the suit of stay-at-home mom to her daughter and two sons (Lily, 12, Landon, 11, and Christian, 2). Ashlee is passionate about sharing her story of healing from abortion with others as a testimony to the hope and forgiveness God offers. She is a believer and follower of Jesus Christ who is active in her church and lives in Port Clinton, Ohio.

Made in the USA
Monee, IL
04 July 2020

35809239R00100